LIFE SAVORS • LIFE SAVORS •

Tyndale House Publishers, Inc.
Carol Stream, Illinois

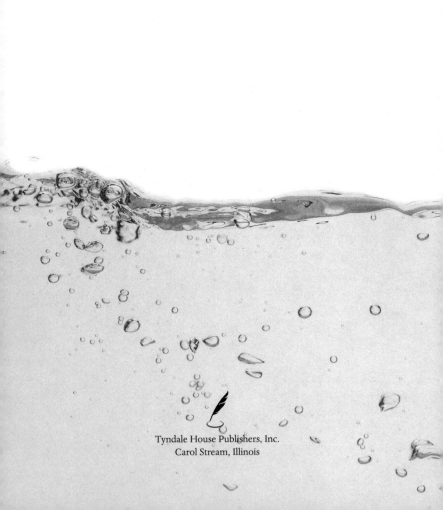

LIFE SAVORS

JAMES STUART BELL
JEANETTE GARDNER LITTLETON

Visit Tyndale's exciting Web site at www.tyndale.com

Life Savors

Designed by Jacqueline L. Nuñez

Edited by Joan Hutcheson

Library of Congress Cataloging-in-Publication Data

Life savors / [edited by] James Stuart Bell and Jeanette Gardner Littleton.
p. cm.
ISBN-13: 978-1-4143-1734-2 (sc)
ISBN-10: 1-4143-1734-4 (sc)
1. Providence and government of God—Christianity—Anecdotes.
2. Christian life—Anecdotes. I. Bell, James Stuart. II. Littleton, Jeanette Gardner.
BT135.L454 2008
248.2—dc22 2007042727

Printed in the United States of America

14 13 12 11 10 09 08
7 6 5 4 3 2 1

Dedication

To Wyatt James Ritchie,
first grandson of a new generation
on life's journey with Jesus

—James Stuart Bell

To the Advisory Board of the Heart of America Christian Writers Network (www.HACWN.org): Sally Danley, Sally Jadlow, Ardy Kolb, Mark Littleton, Patricia Mitchell, Karen Morerod, Phyllis Farringer, and Teresa Vining. These people give constantly to help writers like the ones in this book bless others.

—Jeanette Gardner Littleton

CONTENTS

INTRODUCTION

Life is full of moments to savor—

Restful relaxation with favorite friends . . .

Sights, sounds, and scents of a sweet spring day . . .

The tender touch of someone we truly love.

Such moments bring us hope and peace as we enjoy them with unhurried appreciation. When we take delight in the people and pleasures lacing our days together, we learn to live more fully.

The Christian walk is a savor-full life.

In fact, although the Bible is a user's guide to life, it's not just full of directives and diatribes. Instead, it also includes hundreds of little pictures of people savoring life—from the Old Testament stories of feasts and families and individuals who discovered God's strength, power, and joy as they served him and one another . . . to the portions of Scripture that point out the magnificence of our Father's creation . . . to the snapshots of Jesus laughing, living with, and loving people just like us.

Through these ways and more, the Bible gives us bite-sized pieces of pleasure.

And that's the inspiration for *Life Savors*.

Through this book, we hope that you'll learn to savor

life a little more as forty new friends recount the colorful moments, the challenges, and the watershed events that have added flavor to their lives.

As you read these pages, taste and see that the Lord is good. He's been good in others' lives, and he will bring moments to savor into your life, too.

THE FRIEND AT THE CAFÉ

"You are one *tart*!" I exclaimed, grabbing my friend by the shoulder.

We'd planned to meet at our favorite café at 8 A.M. that morning, but she'd called me, canceling. However, around 1:30 P.M., I felt "impressed" to visit the café.

So there I was, later the same day, sauntering into our mutual stomping ground just because I had an "impression." The place was pretty empty after the lunch rush. And that's when I saw my friend, with her back to me. Her blonde wavy hair rested on the blue T-shirt I'd given her. She was eating her usual meal.

Well, I never! I thought. *She canceled because she wasn't coming to town today, but there she is! I'm really going to give her a hard time.*

That's when I marched over, grabbed her shoulder, and said, "You are one *tart*!"

The face turned to me; it had changed drastically. Confusion washed over it—but nothing compared to the confusion on mine.

"Oh! I'm so sorry," I twittered nervously, as I looked into a stranger's face. What else was I supposed to do in such a situation? Not only had I accosted the poor woman, I had called her a *tart*.

"I . . . I thought you were a friend who stood me up for breakfast this morning," I stuttered. I had to admit it wasn't the first time I'd done something so embarrassing in public. At times I've even conversed with perfect strangers, thinking I knew them. You'd think I'd learn to quit while I'm behind, but no, I keep going! I've even tried to convince them they really were who I thought they were.

Now this woman's blue eyes sparkled, and she laughed. Relief flooded over me. I apologized again and went to the next booth to recover all the equilibrium I'd lost.

Between giggles of embarrassment, I heard an inner voice whisper, *Eileen, you need to go and talk to this woman.*

No, I argued. *How can I do that after making a complete idiot of myself?*

The voice persisted and resisted my excuses. By the time I'd devoured the last of my potatoes, it had become one deafening, almighty shout.

"All right, God! All right!" I heard myself say aloud (another of my embarrassing quirks).

Just then the assailed woman stood to leave. I jumped up and offered my hand.

"I'm so sorry. My name is Eileen, and I feel impressed to talk to you."

She grabbed my hand and squeezed it. "My name is Shelly. This is so very strange."

What an understatement. I invited her to sit.

"Look," I spluttered, "I'm embarrassed about the 'tart' bit. I take it you've never been called that before?"

Her laughter bubbled. "No, I haven't, but I think it's hilarious. You've cheered me up no end."

"It's like this, you see," I started. "I have five sisters, and in Ireland, where I'm from, my sisters and I use the word *tart* to denote a sort of cheeky, fun person."

"Oh! I see."

"Whenever my sisters and I meet each other or talk on the phone, we say, 'Hello, tart.' Since I am the oldest, my sisters often respond, 'Hello, bigger tart.' I do the same thing with my close friends."

Shelly continued laughing. "I think this is just too funny."

"Yes, but I want you to know I don't usually go around doing this kind of thing."

I had the decency to correct myself. "Well, actually, yes I do. Stupid things like this are part of my regular routine."

"Join the club."

I was embarrassed to tell her about the compelling voice I'd heard, instructing me to speak with her. *What if she doesn't even believe in God?* I reasoned. *She might think I am a complete idiot.*

God won. I obeyed his prompting and took the risk.

"I sensed God telling me to talk to you," I blurted, "but I felt like a moron after accosting you like that."

She started to cry.

"Oh no! I haven't done it again, have I?"

"Eileen," she said, touching my hand, "God's taking such good care of me."

She then told me she had come to our town to make arrangements to live nearer her sons.

"You wouldn't believe the last five years of my life." Tears welled again as she paused.

"Shelly, I'm here. I'm listening. God is with us . . . we couldn't have planned this ourselves. Tell me."

"I lost my fifteen-year-old son to an alcohol-related suicide." She gasped for breath.

"I'm so very sorry, Shelly," I whispered, taking her hand in mine.

"His name was Blake. He'd never touched alcohol, but this time he and three school friends went out and shared a large bottle of whiskey."

We let the silence embrace us and reach into our souls.

"His friend Toby went into a coma—alcohol poisoning," she continued. "They took him to the hospital and placed him on life support. When Blake came home, my husband told him to go to his room and wait. My husband went to Toby's house to watch the younger children so Toby's parents could stay at the hospital. They didn't expect Toby to pull through."

A long, poignant pause followed.

"I came home from work and found Blake dead. He had taken the gun from a locked cabinet and shot himself in the head."

Our hands tightened.

"He'd never been depressed, was a great kid, had never gotten into trouble. There just weren't any signs. None. It was just the stupid alcohol."

"How'd you survive something like that, Shelly?" I asked.

"With great difficulty. God was with me. I was so mad at him for a *long* time, but he got me through it. I wouldn't have survived if I hadn't felt him near me every step of the way."

The waitress filled our cups without comment as if sensing the conversation and depth of the exchange.

"I still get angry with God at times, but I'm working on getting over it."

She sipped her coffee, and I watched her move once more to that silent soul place where memories cease to need words.

"My husband was Blake's stepfather. They loved each other and did everything together. He blamed himself for not being there to protect Blake. He couldn't forgive himself, you see. He kept repeating, 'If I'd been here, he wouldn't have died.' He became helpless."

"That's desperate, Shelly." I was too moved to say anything stupid.

"It got worse, Eileen. He decided life wasn't worth living without Blake. He had severe physical challenges, so he took to bed and started dying right in front of me. Part of me felt abandoned. I needed him to be there for me, and he wasn't. I was his caregiver until he died."

Her pain was palpable.

"I lost two of the men in my life because of alcohol. Neither of them drank. Until that night."

"I'm so sorry, Shelly. I can't imagine such pain."

"To make matters worse, his family abandoned me. I haven't seen them since the funeral."

She cried softly; I squeezed her hand.

"I had been very close to his daughters. They thought their father had left a lot of money and that I kept it for myself. He didn't. He had run up debts, remortgaged the house, and didn't have insurance."

She let that sink in. "I had to start all over again. At fifty-two, I was back to square one. The hardest part," she whispered, "was the way his family treated me."

Silence enveloped us.

"Shelly, how *did* you survive all this?"

"God's grace," she whispered. "God's grace."

She wiped her eyes and looked at me. "Eileen, I had three choices. I could lie down and die. Dying seemed an easier option than living. Have you ever felt like that?"

I simply nodded.

"I could choose to blame God and abandon my faith. Or I could trust God and make a new beginning. That's what I did. I retrained in banking and finance. I started over. I'm making plans to move here."

"Wow! You're amazing. Here you were, having a peaceful meal, and I come in and call you a tart!"

Her laughter gurgled. "That's just what I needed. I believe God put you in my path. You're my kind of woman."

We talked more, then exchanged e-mail addresses and phone numbers.

"When you move here, we'll start a Tarts' Breakfast Club and you can meet my 'sister tart.'"

"Count me in. I feel better already."

She shifted gears. "I'm scared. Starting over at fifty-two is not easy."

"I know, Shelly, I know," I said. "I started over at fifty, too. I changed careers after twenty-five years. Then I married for the first time and moved here from London."

"You didn't marry until you were fifty? That's hard to believe."

I agreed.

"You know, Shelly, it's been an awesome and challenging journey. God has really turned my life upside down, and I've learned to trust him at a totally new level."

"What do you mean?" she queried.

"Well, not too long ago, I unexpectedly lost my job in a church. I was shocked when I realized I'd never really trusted

God to take care of me financially. I was always able to take care of things myself."

"Same here," she said. "That's it—the scariest part for me is the financial one."

"God looked after me in incredible ways. I'm still being surprised. I'm learning to open closed-off areas in my heart. I've learned about forgiving myself and others."

"Yes, I feel I've had emotional bypass surgery," she acknowledged. "I've closed parts of my heart too. I know I need to work on forgiveness and releasing resentment. I'm struggling to get there."

"You're doing great, Shelly. Look what you've accomplished. You've survived when others would be crushed."

God, please tell me what else I need to say, I prayed silently. "Maybe you could ask God to help you get to the place where you would be willing and able to start the journey of forgiveness."

"That sounds good. I can take baby steps to get there. God will see me through it."

"He has. He will."

The tables and chairs around us were stacked; the café was closing. Shelly and I hugged and promised to keep in touch.

God has a great sense of humor and can even use a bungler like me for his purposes. I'm slow on the uptake. But I learned, once again, to heed his voice, get over my own embarrassment, and reach out to a stranger who was simply a friend I had yet to meet.

—Eileen Roddy-Phillips

GLORIOUS PEACE

I was nineteen years old the first time my twenty-nine-year-old boyfriend, Rich, said, "I sure wish I had never left the army nine years ago. I believe I will re-enlist."

Fear and insecurity settled into every fiber of my being when he spoke those words. Immediately, I began what I dubbed my "rationalization routine" as though I were trying to talk him out of going off to war instead of simply re-enlisting. "Oh, you can't leave," I would plead, "I am only in my second year of college. The military could send you anywhere, and I would not be able to follow you."

That was only the beginning of my speech. As I rattled on, as desperate people do, he finally tired of listening to me and agreed, for the time anyway, not to re-enlist in the army. I could relax until he mentioned it again.

Finally, he stopped mentioning it. By the time he was thirty-one, we had moved to New England. Rich was engrossed in a successful sales career. I was equally smitten with my new publishing career. Days turned into years, until we finally decided to wed at the ages of thirty-seven and twenty-seven. We had a little girl. We had a little boy. We had a house in the country. And we had an enormous hole in the middle of our lives.

After much soul searching, I began to realize the hole was spiritual. Soon, I attended church every week, put Bible verses on the fridge, and asked if we could let our daughter attend a private Christian school.

The Bible verses were not a huge hit with Rich. The children and I went to church without Daddy. By the grace of God, he conceded to the Christian school idea, though I am convinced that he believed aliens had brainwashed his wife with this "religious" thing.

Several school functions later, Rich developed a heart for Jesus, and the transformation in our home was incredible. Sometime after this transformation, Rich lost a lucrative sales job. At this point, he was forty-two and thinking he never wanted another sales job. What he did want was to make a more obvious difference in someone else's life.

With that line of thinking, we began to pray every day, "Dear Lord, please show us where you want Rich to be. If you want him back in sales, then open that door and guide him, but if you want something else for him, Lord, then show us what that is and give us the peace that surpasses all understanding."

On his forty-third birthday, after months of repeating that same prayer, Rich still had not been offered a job. One day, he was meeting with a local job placement agency. The interview was long, so I thought it must be going very well.

Hours later, I heard his footsteps racing up the stairs two at a time. *Oh, thank you, God,* I thought, breathing a sigh of relief. *He'll have good news.*

He stood in the doorway gazing at the children and me as we played on the floor.

I looked right into his blue eyes and thought, *I don't know what he's about to say, but I know it will be life changing.*

"What is it?" I asked, already feeling an overwhelming sense of peace enter the edges of my mind.

"I just joined the National Guard," he began to explain. "They accepted me at my age because of my previous military experience . . ." His voice trailed off.

"And?" I asked, feeling that peaceful sensation go from my head into the rest of my body, as though it was surfing through my blood vessels. I felt fully prepared for what I was about to hear.

"And I am going to Iraq. I mean, I really hope to go to Afghanistan, but it looks like I'm going to Iraq. Just think, honey, I will be serving my country, and maybe even by going over there, just one soldier who was going for his third or fourth time can stay home with his two little kids for a change, and . . ."

"Go on." I smiled at him, caught up in his enthusiasm.

"Why aren't you trying to talk me out of it, or crying, or angry or something?" he asked, amazed.

"You will think I am insane when I tell you," I replied.

"Try me," he said.

"OK," I began. "I think it is an answer to our prayers, and I think God prepared me for it in the time it took you to come up those stairs and look me in the eye."

Silence filled the room as my response soaked in.

"I told you it sounded crazy," I said.

"No," he said. "All the way home, I just knew it was an answer to our prayers. I just didn't know how to make you see that. Instead, God took care of that for me, and he allowed you to see it in an instant."

Rich recently left for Iraq. He will gladly turn forty-five in Baghdad. He never thought I was crazy, but plenty of other people have thought the two of us are several cards short of a full deck. I have heard it all: "Why didn't you talk him out of it?" "Why didn't you give him some type of ultimatum?" "How could you allow your husband to go at forty-four?"

I try to explain to people that sixteen years ago, I was a faithless, scared little girl, afraid of losing my boyfriend if he enlisted in the army—and no wars were even going on at the time. But now, during wartime, God took away all that fear and replaced it with peace. His peace. I know my husband is exactly where he is supposed to be. I sense the peace that surpasses all understanding. What a glorious experience!

—Melissa Fields

YOU NEVER KNOW WHERE SUCCESS MIGHT TAKE YOU

Soon Number 32 would be announced. We waited for my daughter to run onto the basketball court to play in the final game of her collegiate career. As we waited, my wife leaned over and whispered in my ear, "God is faithful."

"Yes," I replied. "God does work miracles."

"Remember when she prayed to God for a new nose?" my wife asked.

I nodded, as she squeezed my hand and continued, "We prayed she would come to accept the nose God had given her and to praise the Lord for all things, even her nose. Who ever would have believed she would become a college athlete?"

I smiled as I thought about how it all began. My daughter was born with severe asthma and allergies, so none of us believed she could become an athlete. Almost from birth we had to take great care to prevent asthma attacks—including limiting her activities, especially those involving running. By the time she reached school age, she preferred dresses and shiny shoes to gym shorts and tennis shoes. But in third grade, everything changed.

A man came to her classroom just before Christmas vacation to tell the third graders about the Hoop Shoot. Each year, students in third through eighth grade competed in a Hoop-Shoot contest.

My daughter came home excited about participating. She waved her sign-up form in my face, begging me to sign.

"Do you have any idea what you do at a Hoop Shoot?" I asked.

"No," she responded, "but everyone is going to do it."

"You must shoot twenty-five baskets from the foul line," I said. "The one who makes the most baskets wins. Have you ever tried to shoot a basket from the foul line in the high school gym?"

"No," she admitted, "but I still want to do it."

I glanced at my wife, hoping for support, but I got no more than a nod.

I had seen many Hoop-Shoot contests. I have to admit I was more concerned about my daughter's confidence than her asthma. The Hoop-Shoot contest did not involve any running, but it did require athletic skill.

As a former high school coach, I subscribed to a philosophy of building confidence in beginning athletes by allowing them to be successful while they were learning the skills of a sport. I felt the Hoop Shoot did the opposite. Little third-grade girls were required to shoot a basket with a high school basketball in a high school gymnasium. I felt those third graders should shoot at a shorter basket and from a closer distance. I often grimaced as I watched pint-sized hoopsters throw basketball after basketball hopelessly short of the mark. Not only that, but the third graders had to compete against the older, stronger, and more-experienced fourth graders—another confidence deflator because the older girls almost always won.

I was convinced this system did not build successful

basketball skills or players, but I couldn't say no to my determined daughter. I signed the form. She promptly tucked it in her backpack.

Not long after Christmas vacation, the night for the Hoop Shoot arrived. Neither my wife nor I had marked the date on our calendars and had scheduled important meetings for the evening. My daughter said nothing about the matter until the babysitter arrived.

"Who's going to take me to the Hoop Shoot?" my daughter asked.

"What?" I responded.

"Tonight is the Hoop Shoot," she said. "Don't you remember?"

My wife and I looked helplessly at each other.

"I can take her," the babysitter offered.

"But it's been snowing all day," I protested. "It's still snowing and a bad night to be outdoors."

"It's only a few blocks," the babysitter noted. "Really, it's no problem."

"Please, Dad," my daughter pleaded.

"Oh, all right," I said. "I guess you can go."

I was upset with myself for not being there for my daughter. As a school administrator, I often preach on the importance of parental involvement to a child's development. So I was anxious to get home after my meeting, knowing I could at least encourage her.

"Dad!" my daughter exclaimed as I came through the door. "I won!"

"What?" I asked.

"Jessica and I tied," she shouted. "I made a basket. We both won the contest."

"Wow, that's great!" I declared.

Whether it was because of the bad weather or not I never knew, but the next day I learned that of the younger competitors, only my daughter and her best friend had turned out for the competition.

Both girls had helplessly lobbed twenty-five underhand shots at the basket, making only one basket each. The officials decided to see if they could break the tie by letting each girl have ten more shots at the basket, but each made only one more basket.

I could just imagine the hapless volunteers as they conducted the Hoop Shoot. Twenty or thirty older students would have stood around, anxiously waiting for their turn, watching in agony as the youngest girls threw basketball after basketball short of the mark. I could almost hear the groans.

The officials had decided to call it a tie after the shoot-off, and so my daughter, who did not know how to shoot a basket before entering the gym that night, left as a winner in the third- and fourth-grade division of the local Hoop-Shoot contest.

"I need you to sign this form for the regional Hoop Shoot," my daughter shouted as she waved a new form in front of me.

"Regional Hoop Shoot?"

I agreed to sign her slip, but I told her we would have to go to the gym and practice before she could go to regionals.

The regionals took place in a town about an hour's drive from our rural community. In winter, the two-lane road along the twisting river was one I avoided, especially if it was snowing.

My knuckles were white by the time we reached the

Hoop Shoot that day. The snow had fallen steadily all morning. I didn't hold much hope that my daughter would be successful at this level, and I somewhat resented having to make the dangerous trip.

I put on a brave front and told my daughter, "There are no losers here. Everyone had to win at the local level to be here. So, you just go out there and do your best. Remember to be a good sport, dear."

"Don't worry, Dad," she said with a confident smile. "I'll do my best."

I patted her on the back before she ran off to join the other third- and fourth-grade contestants.

She was the first one to the line. She made seven baskets. *Well, that was something,* I thought. She and I watched other girls take their turns. One by one the other contestants failed to match my daughter's seven baskets. Finally, the last girl, clearly a fourth-grader and an athlete, was at the line. She missed her first few shots and then connected. She made another. Missed several more. Made another. Four . . . five . . . six . . . That was it. My daughter had won?

I watched my beaming third grader pose for her picture with her trophy for the local paper. After the picture I saw an official hand my daughter another consent form.

"How far does this thing go?" I asked the official.

"The state contest is in Boise, the Northwest regional is in Montana this year, and the nationals are in Chicago."

"Snow areas," I sighed, as I signed the form allowing my daughter to participate in the state finals.

More practice and a few weeks later, I awoke to near-blizzard conditions, but I knew that regardless of the weather, I would be taking one regional Hoop-Shoot champion to the state contest. We found the high school and entered a whole new world of Hoop-Shoot winners. Clearly, the state contest was more intense than even I had imagined.

Thirty little third- and fourth-grade girls lined up for instructions. Most wore matching outfits. Anxious parents held clipboards with tracking sheets for each contestant. After the instructions, the girls had the court to themselves. As the contestants took their final practice shots, I noticed my daughter was not warming up. She was going around to each contestant introducing herself, shaking hands, and wishing each good luck. I could not have been prouder.

My daughter did not win that day, although she improved to making eight out of twenty-five baskets. As she skipped toward me, I tried to decide what to say to my daughter. I wanted to say something uplifting, something to encourage her. I wanted to tell her how proud I was of her sportsmanship. But before I could say a word, she bounced up to me and hugged my leg. "Don't worry, Dad, I'll be back next year."

At that moment I knew the love of the sport had taken hold of her. I knew the seeds of success were planted.

Over the years, those seeds were nurtured by other successful efforts, and now I sat as Number 32 ran onto the basketball court for her final college game. I smiled, thinking, *You never know where God and a little success might take you.*

—Michael J. Keown

YES, WE HAVE NO BANANAS

I flattened myself against the wall as the teeming sea of teenagers flowed by. Other teachers and I watched for fights that sometimes erupted as students jostled one another.

"Mr. Gray! Over by the stairs!" I yelled, when I glimpsed our assistant principal.

The urban high school where I taught students with learning disabilities required adults to patrol the five floors between classes. We also watched for kids roaming the halls during class. Some days peace prevailed. However, on too many other days, tension, anger, and adolescence reigned.

I discovered an island of refreshment from the barely contained chaos: the weekly Youth for Christ meeting. After a few meetings, I got to know the hearts of several dedicated young people, as well as the hearts of the sponsors, Diane and Mary.

"Could we visit the nursing home up the street?" one of the students, Cynthia, asked at the end of September. "We could sing, and Aaron or Cortez could preach."

"Sure," Diane said. "You call the administrators of the home and find out if they'd like us to come."

The kids caught the vision for ministry and voted for a monthly visit. The outreach depended on two conditions:

the nursing home's OK and parental permission to ride in our cars. Both were met by the next week's meeting.

The students planned a program each month. They opened with a few praise choruses and then led the residents in old hymns. Even residents who appeared unaware of their surroundings joined in for familiar songs. Then one of the young men preached a minisermon to our congregation of the old and broken down. After a closing prayer, each of us visited with individual residents.

"I need prayer," said an elderly man whose wheelchair sat on the fringe of the crowd.

"Please pray for my grandson," said a tiny, white-haired lady who was almost hidden behind her walker.

Other residents simply waited for a kind word, a hug, or a pat on a wrinkled arm. We overlooked shaking heads and hands and ignored the occasional drool. Frequently, one or two residents rewarded us with sweet smiles and said, "Thank you."

After the Thanksgiving break, student, Shenequa, said, "Let's take gifts to the nursing home for Christmas."

"What a great idea," said Diane. "Would you call the home's administrator about an appropriate gift?"

The administrator suggested ripe bananas. All the residents could eat the soft, sweet fruit and considered them special treats. We were a little surprised at the request, but every student and adult agreed to bring a bunch of bananas on the day of the Christmas visit.

I brought a big white bag to hold the bananas on the day of our Christmas program. Our group met with anticipation—and only three bunches of bananas.

"How can we go without enough bananas? There can't

be more than fifteen or sixteen in our bag," I worried, because I knew thirty residents could show up for our visit. But we didn't have time to buy more bananas before going to the nursing home.

Diane's raised eyebrows signaled her concern as well. She whispered, "Maybe there won't be so many people today."

"Maybe we should just forget it," Mary said quietly.

But we'd promised to go, so we walked to our cars with heavy hearts. None of the students seemed aware of the shortfall as they crawled into the three vehicles.

Our hopes for fewer people evaporated when we entered the community room, packed with thirty or more residents. We adults knew our white bag of bananas could never feed them all.

After the service, a staff member stood behind a counter with the bag of bananas. The residents walked or rolled up, one at a time, to receive their gifts. Our students carefully escorted each of them to the counter and then back to their seats.

"I just love bananas!" one little lady exclaimed.

"Me, too," said two or three others who were awaiting their turns.

Another resident presented himself for a banana—and received one. Yet another ambled to the counter, and there was one more banana. This process continued.

"Do you see what I see?" I asked Diane. "The staff didn't bring out any more bananas, did they?"

Diane shook her head, while she kept her eyes glued to the banana bag.

Though we certainly hadn't brought enough bananas, the staff person pulled out one more golden banana from the white bag . . . and one more . . . and one more . . . until every resident in the room clasped a banana. Even the gentleman asleep on the bed would get his when he woke up.

Quietly Diane and I laughed. We cried. We even danced a little!

No one seemed aware of our glee. None of the residents seemed to have a clue what had taken place that day, and only one or two of the young people recognized the pitiful number of bananas.

"Do you remember how many bananas we took with us today?" I asked the kids as we rode back to school.

Aaron spoke up, "I was just thinking about that. We didn't take enough, did we?"

"We couldn't have. We took only three small bunches," Shenequa said.

"We just happened to have the exact number of bananas," said Aaron.

"'Just happened' to? I don't think so."

The kids continued talking about the visit. As soon as we parked, students spilled out of all three cars. One yelled, "Did you see it? Did you see what God did to those bananas?"

"Nobody got left out. Not a single one!" said another.

The excitement was contagious—more dancing and laughter. We shared one big, noisy hug right in the school parking lot before we all left for our homes in awe and wonder.

I'm still not certain what happened that day. Maybe I underestimated the number of bananas, or maybe just the right number of residents attended. Or, maybe the bananas did multiply.

Whatever happened, I believe we saw God's heart that Christmas. He blanketed us all—weakened elderly, service-minded students, and surprised teachers—with his pure love.

—Linda Holloway

FACING FEAR

Thud! Thud! The bats swooped under the eaves and repeatedly banged against the window. With each jarring *thump,* I was sure the glass would shatter and they would be upon me, rabid eyes wild, sharp fangs bared, thirsty for my blood. I pulled the sheet up around my neck to protect me from the sting of bites that would soon come. . . .

I wasn't allowed to watch the Saturday afternoon *Creature Feature* again. My parents were certain that watching Dracula caused my nightmares. I wasn't so sure. I'd long been afraid of the shadows that danced on my wall after good-night kisses and bedtime prayers. And no one else in the third grade admitted to sleeping with a night-light.

As I grew, my fears grew along with me. I left behind the fear of make-believe monsters, trading it for a terror of being left alone. If my parents left me in the car while they ran errands, I was sure I would be kidnapped and buried alive like the girl I'd read about in *Reader's Digest.* When they dropped me off at summer camp, I was certain they'd move while I was gone, and I'd never see them again.

But against the backdrop of teenage angst, my fears seemed to mellow. In Sunday school, I memorized many

Scripture passages about fear, and I learned to draw on them when afraid.

As a young adult I fell in love and married a handsome young helicopter pilot. That's when I noticed how many helicopters seemed to crash. The evening news, the morning paper, everywhere I turned, I saw pictures of wrecked aircraft and captions reading, "No Survivors!"

Late one night when my husband, Derek, hadn't returned from a mission, I was forced to confront this fear. I didn't want to spend my married life afraid every time my husband walked out the door. As a Christian, I knew God required me to trust him implicitly. Did I really believe my faith was enough to sustain me if I lost Derek? Was God big enough to help me face this fear?

After a long night of prayer and soul searching, I came to a place of deeper faith. I believed God's Word. If God was with Jonah in the belly of the whale, with Daniel in the lions' den, and with Job when he lost all he held dear, then surely he would be with Derek in the cockpit of his helicopter and with me as I waited for his return. By the time my husband walked through the door, I'd found renewed peace.

In the following years, we were blessed with three healthy sons. I thought I had vanquished my enemy of the night. All the bumps, bruises, and sicknesses of raising boys gave me ample opportunity to stretch my faith.

On September 24, 1999, after an uneventful pregnancy and speedy delivery, I gave birth to our fourth son. He was born with congenital diaphragmatic hernia, a life-threatening birth defect with a 50–80 percent mortality rate. Early in gestation, a hole in his diaphragm had not closed as it should have. His intestinal organs had pushed up into his lung cavity, squashing his developing lungs.

He was flown by helicopter to a local hospital immediately after birth. He looked beautiful and healthy. He fought the paramedics who tried to hook him up to monitors and IVs, quieting only when he heard my voice. As the crew wheeled him away, the flight nurse turned to me. "You need to understand that your baby is very, very sick," she said. "The next time you see him, he won't look like this."

I returned to the room where I'd given birth less than an hour before. I crawled into the bed, turned my back on the bassinet, and closed my eyes. All through that endless day and even longer night, I assimilated facts and information as the neonatalogist called from my son's room. My husband had gone with the baby, but my doctor wouldn't discharge me so quickly after giving birth.

Visitors came and prayed and left. Our three little boys came to see me, wondering where the new baby was, and at last the nurses turned down the lights. Three of us were in the room that night: me, the Lord, and Fear.

Numbed and exhausted, I pulled my Bible out of my overnight bag. Too overwhelmed to read, I opened it to Psalms and laid it on my chest, hoping to gain comfort from the nearness of its pages. "Lord, you are asking me to face the one thing I cannot face. But if your plan for me is to experience the disability or death of my son, you will have to help me—this is too big for me."

The following morning I went to see my baby, Sam. I'm not sure what could have prepared me for the sight of my child that day. He was in a medically induced coma, so fragile that the touch of my finger on his toe raised his blood pressure to a critical level. We had to whisper because the sound of our voices was too stressful for his delicate system. We could only wait to see if he would stabilize so he could have the surgery he desperately needed. I went home that night and saw his empty cradle at the foot of our bed. I cried.

When Sam was three days old, he had surgery to repair the hernia and came through beautifully. After he had been in the neonatal intensive-care unit for three weeks, we were able to take him home. I hoped the worst was over and that we would live happily ever after. I was wrong.

I thought fear was a familiar foe, but it was nothing compared to the mind-numbing, energy-sapping battle I now found myself engaged in.

Surgery had corrected Sam's birth defect, but risks and complications are associated with this particular disorder. He had just one lung. The doctors were cautiously optimistic; I was unabashedly terrified.

If Sam was fussy, I was sure he had an intestinal blockage. If he wouldn't nurse, I feared reherniation. If he cried, I despaired of his getting enough oxygen with his one tiny lung. Numb with depression and sick with fear, I couldn't seem to enjoy all the precious things we once doubted we'd experience. His first smile, first bath, first giggle were colored with my fear. I lived each day waiting for the other shoe to drop.

On New Year's Eve, Sam was fussy. He spat up a lot and fussed when he nursed. I called the doctor's office and was told it was probably just an upset tummy. I wished I could have believed them, but I didn't.

A winter storm was raging the last day of 1999. I drove slowly to the corner grocery to get some medicine for Sam, made my purchase, and dashed back to the car. As I sat behind the wheel, the nameless dread rose within me, and all the fear I thought I'd conquered broke over me in waves of terror.

I couldn't live another minute dreading Sam's death.

In the deserted parking lot, I cried out to God. Did I really believe God was good? All these years I'd tried so hard to trust him. But fear and faith can't exist side by side. I'd struggled so many years to be free, yet when it came to what was most precious to me, I found I really didn't trust God after all.

I began to speak aloud Scripture I'd memorized as a child. And I prayed, "O God, I choose to believe that you are good even though you're allowing me to walk through my deepest fear. I know your character as revealed through your Word. It is impossible for you to do evil. If you choose to take Sam from me, I promise you I will say, 'The Lord gave me what I had, and the Lord has taken it away. Praise the name of the Lord!'"

There. I had spoken it. My fear was exposed and lying before me in the cold winter light. And I knew that even if Sam were to die, I would live.

Peace descended as I sat in the snow-covered parking lot. The knot in my stomach eased for the first time since Sam's birth. I would not let fear steal one more minute from me. Whatever the years brought, I would choose to face them with faith instead of fear.

I drove home and welcomed the year 2000 with my family. We were the first ones in the urgent-care clinic the next morning. After a careful exam, the pediatrician said, "This little guy's got his first ear infection."

I wept with relief.

That same week, Sam's surgeon requested new X-rays

and made an amazing discovery. At the time of his surgery, X-rays had revealed a few tiny pieces of tissue called lung "buds" where his left lung should have been. The doctors hoped that during the next fourteen years, these buds would grow enough to form a partially functioning lung. The new X-rays showed that only three months later, God was answering prayers that I couldn't even pray. Sam had miraculously grown a fully functioning left lung.

I can't say I never struggled with fear again, but faith is like a muscle that grows stronger when exercised. When circumstances arise that make my faith shaky, I sit down with a photo album. I look at the pictures of a baby with tubes and monitors attached to every part of his body, and then I go to the window and look outside at the sturdy seven-year-old roughhousing with his brothers. I serve a God who loves me enough to turn my weaknesses into strength. The name we'd chosen for this son before his birth is so appropriate—Samuel, "God has heard."

—Cindy Hval

THE CHRISTMAS CARD

"Why do people send store-bought Christmas cards?" I overheard a young woman say, as I waited in line for a table at a busy Mexican restaurant one day in December.

"I mean, who wants a card with a printed message and just a name written on the bottom?" she continued. "It's not very personal. I don't want to send a card unless I can write it myself, with my own message. And I just don't have time for that with the shopping and the decorating and all. I don't imagine anyone else does, either, so why bother?"

Her words seemed so unknowing to me. I wanted to tell her that she'd be surprised what a Christmas card can mean.

Years before, on a Sunday afternoon a few weeks before Christmas, I sat at my dining room table hurriedly working on my Christmas card list, which included family, friends, and employees of the restaurant we owned. The card I had chosen that year featured a picture of a shepherd watching over his sheep, contemplating the starry night sky over Bethlehem.

Suddenly, I had a sense of doubt about what I was doing. I wondered if this was how God wanted me to spend my money. Adding together the cost of the cards and postage, I had spent over one hundred dollars. What if God wanted me to give that hundred dollars to a foreign mission or to our church, instead?

I bowed my head and prayed, *Lord, is this what you wanted me to do with this money? Or did you have other plans for it? I really wish you would let me know. I would like to have peace about how I've spent these funds.*

Then I picked up my pen and finished the cards.

Shortly before Christmas, I was working at my desk at the back of the restaurant dining room when Sidney pushed open the swinging door from the kitchen and shuffled toward me. Sidney was our night dishwasher. He was a small, thin man with gray hair and the wrinkled face of a lifetime smoker. Sidney had lived a hard life as a merchant marine, and he looked older than his fifty-odd years.

Sidney drank too much and periodically checked into the state hospital to dry out. He lived in a small camping trailer, the kind you pull behind a car or truck. His brother, whom he sometimes got along with, had let him put the trailer in the backyard of a house he rented out to someone else. Sid had no family except for this brother and his niece, Valerie, who waited tables for us and had helped him get this dishwashing job. Sid was slow, and I was often frustrated when I had to stay late while he finished, but he was always cheerful. Now, smiling and drying his hands on his stained apron, he approached me. As I continued checking over an invoice, I wondered vaguely what this interruption would be about.

"Sally," he started, "I want to thank you for the Christmas card you sent me." Continuing to wring his hands in his apron, he said, "You know, people like me don't get many Christmas cards."

My throat tightened as I realized the truth of his statement.

"And you know what?" he said as his face broke into a gaping grin, "I used to be a shepherd, too, just like Jesus. I watched them sheep day and night, pulled 'em outta bushes, herded 'em to fresh water, sheared 'em when their coats was too long, kept the coyotes away. I know what it means to be a shepherd, just like Jesus. Now, ain't that somethin'?"

Averting his eyes and twisting the apron in his hands, he finished. "Well, I just wanted to say thanks, Sally. It meant a lot to me."

Struggling to find my voice, I answered, "You're welcome, Sid."

I was struck silent, as I often am when I hear God's voice. As Sid turned to walk back to the dish room, he missed the tear that slid down my cheek. The store-bought Christmas card I had sent out that year had meant the most to one of the least-important people on my list.

I suddenly saw Sidney through Jesus' eyes and knew I had the answer to my prayer. God used my hundred dollars to remind a lonely, used-up man that he was not forgotten by his Shepherd. God reminded Sidney that he was watching over him, and he spoke to Sidney in just the right way to touch his heart and to connect with him. Then God used Sidney's words to teach me that God's love is as great for the ordinary and the troubled as it is for foreign missionaries and religious institutions.

Sidney worked for us for almost a year after that, until one day he didn't show up for work. Valerie said he was back in the state hospital, and I never saw him again. A year or two after that, Sid passed away of emphysema. Valerie said he died trusting that Jesus was with him, just like a good shepherd would be.

I cried when she told me, and I said a prayer of thanks

to have known this man and for what God taught me because of him.

I've never forgotten Sidney. I send out Christmas cards every year, personal or not—they are all personal to God.

—Sally Clark

ACCEPTING GOD'S PROVISION

"You idiot!" Dad shouted at me. "God *is* trying to provide for you!"

I'd pushed Dad to the point of exasperation. But still I wouldn't listen.

I was a twenty-six-year-old, married graduate student and the part-time pastor of a small church. My wife and I had been married for three and a half years. We'd managed to keep the wolf from the door, even though we'd made two major moves in that time, and I'd started a church and studied at three seminaries in three cities.

But now we had a baby on the way, and our eighteen-year-old monster of a car was in trouble. The car looked OK but was enormous and was a lumbering ox to drive. It was an Oldsmobile Super 88 with multiple problems. Some of those problems were just nuisances: The car had a wonky heater—I had to make like a gymnast and stand on my head and suck on a pencil-thin black hose under the dashboard to get the heater to blow warm air onto our feet.

Other problems with the car were serious: The engine ran rough because it had one or two stuck valves. It got only about nine miles per gallon out on the highway—pretty bad, even for those days. I carried a set of jumper cables with me, not so that I could be a Good Samaritan and help others but for those times when the Olds 88 wouldn't start. And the transmission growled ominously.

At Thanksgiving time, my wife and I traveled to my parents' home. Our old red car with the rust spot on the roof got us there, and we had a great time with my family. Everyone asked questions about our church, my progress in school, and our long-term plans. We enjoyed talking about our soon-to-be-born child. But my dad was interested in something else.

"Let's go for a ride," he said. He and I climbed into my red and white tank. Dad gave directions, and a few minutes later we pulled up in front of a car dealership.

He'd spotted a car that he thought would be a good replacement for mine. It was smaller, the odometer had a lot fewer miles than our car, and it would get good gas mileage. It was years old—not decades old like ours was. And Dad had researched the car enough to believe that the dealer had it priced at a discount.

"He doesn't know what he has," Dad grinned. "It's a great buy."

Back at the house I said, "Dad, I can't afford to buy a car."

"Oh, I understand that," he said. "Your mom and I want to buy it for you."

Caught off guard, I stuttered, stammered, and finally said, "No."

After all, I was an adult, a married man with a baby on the way. I almost had a master's degree. I preached to a congregation every week. My ego was burned by the fact that my father thought I needed him to buy me a car. I was willing to ignore the fact that it was true.

We talked. We discussed. We argued for an hour.

Finally, in a fit of spiritual logic, I said, "Look, I believe that God will provide me a car when I need one."

That's when Dad shouted.

"You idiot!" Dad bellowed. "God *is* trying to provide for you. Now, right now, you need a car, and God is giving you one."

But then, right then, emotion overruled insight, and I wouldn't admit that my father's wisdom was better than mine. It didn't help that at one point he laughed, clapped his hands, and said, "Ha! I've got you now. You know I'm right!"

No one in our family was fond of losing arguments. Dad was a bright, strong, articulate person. In the end, the only way I could win was to refuse his offer. I couldn't beat his reasoning, but I could beat him for stubbornness. So, I did. My wife and I rumbled home in our sad, old, four-door sedan.

Eight weeks later our son was born. One day later, the car's transmission began to give up the ghost. Reverse went first, so when I went to get my wife and baby boy from the hospital, I was careful not to park where I would need to back up. When we got to our duplex, I couldn't park in the garage because I wouldn't be able to back out. And the next day, I could tell that the forward gears were not right either.

I was in trouble. Hospital bills loomed, and my wife had given up her job. We depended on what income I could produce. I had accepted a second part-time job, but it still wasn't enough for us to buy a car.

Oh man, I hated it, but I had only one choice. I don't remember what I said when I called Dad, but my speech was steeped in humility.

Dad refrained from saying "I told you so." Instead, he checked to see if the car we'd looked at was still available.

But, of course, it had already been sold. Someone else was enjoying that car. The car dealer had nothing to compare with it, and according to Dad, everything else on the lot was overpriced.

So, I did three things: First, I apologized to Dad, admitting my mistake. Next, I checked the price of getting a fully repaired transmission put into the old car, and I quickly ruled that out. Third, I began to pray, asking the Lord to take over this problem and help us.

Word spread about our crisis. A new baby at home and no car! Plenty of folks were concerned. And God worked, answering our prayers. My wife's granddaddy, a generous Christian man, offered his car to us. He'd heard our car had died and decided it was time he got a new car. It was a gracious act.

I knew what his car was like, having seen it before, but it wouldn't have mattered if I'd known nothing about it. As long as it ran, I would take it. Like our broken-down car, his was also a large four-door sedan, but that was OK. It had a strange, persistent knock in the engine. But the heater worked, and the car drove both forward and in reverse. We were grateful to accept it.

I'd had a lifelong problem with receiving gifts, but God began to show me that my problem was pride. I began to understand that when people offer to do something nice for me, the best thing might be to let them.

"Yes" might be a sign of humility, and "No" might be based on presumption. I learned that faith in God is sometimes expressed by accepting help from others. God's help can come from someone who is close to you.

Granddaddy's car ran a little over a year. Then one day it

wouldn't start, and it never ran again. So, we needed another car. But my father was still there for us. This time he didn't buy us a car. Instead, Dad offered to help us get a loan to buy one. I was learning—this time, I said, "Yes."

—Brad Dixon

THE PINCH PERSPECTIVE

Unless my husband and I smell smoke or hear glass break, we usually don't pay much attention to our kids' bickering. Recently, though, we noticed our daughter Kristin reacting peculiarly toward her older brother, Jordan, who was taunting her with normal sibling stuff such as, "I got the last Pop Tart" or "The dog loves me more than you."

While he teased, we watched Kristin raise her thumb and forefinger about an inch apart, frame Jordan's head between them, squint one eye, then calmly and with vengeful pleasure compress her fingers like she was snuffing out a flame. She then turned smugly and left him standing there with a half-finished wisecrack. Big brothers live for this stuff, but we all cracked up this time.

Noting how effective the technique was for Kristin, the rest of us started "pinching" our daily irritants. I suppose it feels so good because it keeps annoyances in perspective. Once you miniaturize a problem, it becomes laughable and loses its power to frustrate.

Of course, "the pinch" doesn't work on every problem. I remember one Christmas season when we experienced a death in the family and other personal trials crashed in on us like unwelcome guests. I couldn't run, hide, or snuff out my pain; I had to live right through it.

Lying awake one sad, lonely night, I remembered Philippians 4:6-8: "Don't worry about anything; instead, pray about everything. Tell God what you need, and thank him for all he has done. Then you will experience God's peace, which exceeds anything we can understand. His peace will guard your hearts and minds as you live in Christ Jesus. . . . Fix your thoughts on what is true, and honorable, and right, and pure, and lovely, and admirable. Think about things that are excellent and worthy of praise."

I felt my faith strengthen: I couldn't escape suffering, but I could still have peace. Even though it seems to be a contradiction, pain and peace are not mutually exclusive, if you have the right perspective.

Perspective. It's about not worrying but being honest with God about what you need. It's about focusing on what you're thankful for. It's about fixing your thoughts on high things. It's about being aware of what you've learned and about applying what you know is right. It's about opening yourself up to God's peace.

I am resolved not to sweat the small things in life—I'll just "pinch" them! And even through more serious trials, I'll remember that the summer of life inevitably slips into winter, when the grand picnic will be remembered either as the battle against the flies or the feast of sweet strawberries, depending on your perspective.

—Linda Crow

THE GUCCI SALE

If there had been an organization called Clueless People from America, you can be sure I'd have been chosen as its poster child. I affectionately call one year the "year of the Gucci bag."

I'll admit I was never one to be terribly fashion forward or to care about expensive accessories. But it seemed that all the other wives on the entire military base in northern Italy had bought a Gucci handbag at some amazing sale in Florence's open-air market. That's all they talked about for weeks, and they encouraged me to go.

Honestly, not one of those handbags struck me as particularly attractive. But my friends convinced me that leaving a five-year tour in Italy without a Gucci bag was akin to leaving Spain without a Lladr figurine, or Germany without a cuckoo clock.

Besides, who was I to pass up a blue-light special, in any language?

So, off I went to Florence, armed with my friends' trusty directions.

Arriving in town center, I snaked my way through a crowded marketplace littered with multicolored kiosks and enormous tents—each crammed with mountains of fresh produce, trinkets, and other wares. Every gadget imaginable was on display—some the object of boisterous bartering, flailing hands, and occasionally flaring tempers.

Over the din, I heard a voice in my head say, *Remember the Gucci bag.*

Slowly and furtively, I unfolded the paper in my pocket as if it were a treasure map. It began simply:

1. Go to fruit stand.
2. Ask for Giuseppe. . . .

I'm no brain surgeon, but I was smart enough to know this did not look promising. To my way of thinking, it was like walking the streets of Seoul, Korea, looking for a certain dark-haired man named Mr. Kim. But I persevered.

Eventually, my persistence paid off. Here was the designated fruit stand, with Giuseppe heading toward me. I promptly glanced at the final directive on my "map." It read,

3. Whisper "Gucci!"

So I did. Now, you'd presume that the word *whisper* would have been my first clue that something was amiss. But no. I'm clueless, remember? Otherwise, wouldn't I have also noticed there was no blue light at this special or wondered why a fruit man would be selling ladies' purses?

Before I could ponder these questions further, Giuseppe was beside me, looking much like Peter Sellers in his Inspector Clouseau role—twitching his bushy mustache, rolling his shifty eyes from left to right without moving his head, pulling up the collar of his trench coat. . . .

Suddenly, I didn't care if I were the only person in the world without a Gucci bag. Just let me buy a couple of kumquats, we'll call it even, and I'll depart with a friendly "ciao" and a handshake.

But it was too late. Already, Giuseppi was leading me through the crowd, away from the market, down one remote alleyway, and through another. When we reached a large, nondescript door, he stealthily scanned the alley while thrusting a key into the lock. My heart thumped and my mind raced as the massive door squeaked on its hinges and opened. He motioned me inside, quickly bolting the door behind us.

There, in a dimly lit warehouse, were hundreds—probably thousands—of the ugliest handbags I'd ever seen. Guccis of every shape, color, size, and style imaginable . . . shelf upon shelf, row upon row . . . stacked to the ceiling, as far as the eye could see.

Surely this was some bizarre nightmare, and I'd wake up gripping my pillow like a clutch bag.

"S-o-o-o . . . whatta you want, lade-e-e?" he uttered in low tones, which was unnecessary because no one could have heard, even if one of us had screamed. (That would have been me.)

"Whatta you want?" he repeated, with more salesman-like insistence this time.

I want my mommy was my immediate thought.

No telling how long we were in there. I only know I must have set an all-time record for a red-blooded American female deciding on a purchase in a handbag store. As long as they were all ugly, what did it really matter, anyway? Just surprise me, and let's get out of here!

Grabbing a motley-brown, squarish one with a long, camel-colored strap, I unrolled my wad of lire, handed over all the cash he asked for, and stood trembling by the door like a puppy eager to go outside.

Daylight never looked so good. My getaway car never looked so good. And my Gucci bag never . . . well, to be honest, it never did feel *or* look all that good . . . so it never made it out of the shopping bag. It stayed in the back of my closet, to remind me now and then of an important life principle.

Someday I'll figure out what that would be—perhaps something like this: "She who seeks blue light . . . and finds black market . . . could end up in red puddle." This escapade could have easily ended in tragedy. We clueless people usually mean well; we're just long on naïveté, short on common sense. Honestly, if I were a guardian angel assigned to me, I'd be lobbying for an easier assignment—like guarding a daredevil hang glider or a bull runner with a death wish.

So often we can get ourselves into what Grandma used to call "pickle jams." Is that a passionate "Amen!" coming from you? Are we kindred spirits in this? We look back on times we did dumb things—or even wrong things, like cluelessly buying Gucci bags that were probably stolen or at least illegal duplicates—and survived. How? Why? For whatever reason, God's protective hand was upon us, pure and simple. We were clueless about that, too.

God's protective hand is on all of us, day in and day out—yet we're usually oblivious to it all. I don't believe it's luck, or coincidence, or random chance that guards and guides my life. I believe it is divine intervention.

Did pilgrims on the *Mayflower* say, "Wow, how lucky!" when one of their own miraculously survived being thrown overboard during a terrible storm? No, in fact Miles Standish declared it was "by the providence of God" that "Beloved Pilgrim John Howland" survived. God had plans for him, which included ten children and generations of grandchildren after that, including my sisters and me. We're grateful for God's hand of protection on "Grandfather John."

When a drunk driver going ninety-five miles an hour hit me, the impact sent my driver-side door careening through the air. The highway patrol reported that had the other driver been going a mile an hour faster, or I, a mile an hour slower, I would have been hit broadside and met an instant death. Had I not inadvertently unbuckled my seat belt moments earlier, I would have rolled with the car into the ravine instead of being thrown to safety onto the highway. Had the first person on the scene not been an off-duty ambulance driver who treated me for shock, who knows where I would be today? I was twenty-one, and not yet a Christian. I believe God mercifully spared my life for a purpose.

He has surely done the same for you. You and I, not knowing the length of our days, are to "realize the brevity of life, so that we may grow in wisdom" (Psalm 90:12).

Grow in wisdom. Sounds good. Sure wish I'd done that when the blue-light special called my name. But I'm thankful my survival was not dependent on my wisdom or the lack of it that morning. And if I'm ever tempted to question the gracious, protective, sovereign hand of God in my life, I need only reach into the back of my closet, unearth that old motley-brown Gucci handbag, and remember the day he spared his clueless daughter from harm.

In the Bible, God calls those who are faithful to him "my own special treasure." He says, "I will spare them as a father spares an obedient child" (Malachi 3:17).

Is that not incredible? Faithful children never need to go seeking special treasure in some marketplace. They'll find it in the Father's heart, where it's been all along.

—Sandi Banks

SHE'S ONLY FOURTEEN

"Lord, isn't this a bit extreme? Isn't there another way? She's only fourteen!"

I'd prayed for our daughter to develop a real hunger for spiritual truth, and now she thought the Lord wanted her to go to Haiti. Haiti! Could this be the answer to my prayer? Seven weeks away from home in a land of poverty that actively practices voodoo? It sounded more like her idea than God's.

Excuses to keep her home flooded my mind: What about her dentist appointments? It was almost time for her braces to come off. My husband, Rick, and I talked it over and decided God would close the door of opportunity if he didn't want her to go. I rested in the fact that twelve hundred dollars for expenses seemed an unlikely amount for her to pull together. We stepped forward in faith.

The money started coming in. One night, I walked in the door from work and waved three more checks under my husband's nose.

"How much?"

I stared at the support checks my coworkers had donated. "Seventy-five dollars."

I'd helped Heather draft a letter to send out asking for support, but I didn't do it for her. If she wanted to go, she'd have to do the work. To my surprise, she wrote the letters out by hand, addressed the envelopes, and mailed them.

We made an appointment for her medical checkup, and the doctor gave her a clean bill of health. He updated her immunizations, and we filled the prescription for malaria meds. Reading the label on the vial of big round pills filled me with apprehension.

"Will you be able to swallow these things?" I asked.

"Oh, Mom. If I have to, I'll cut them in half," she assured me.

She had a hard time swallowing aspirin. Now she'd be thousands of miles away thwarting life-threatening diseases with medication the size of horse pills I didn't know if she could swallow. Where was my faith?

I walked in the door that night to the savory aroma of green peppers, tomatoes, and beef. Heather had dinner ready most nights. It was hard to believe she'd be so far away, for so long. What kind of food would she be eating? I prayed for sanitary cooking conditions.

After dinner we totaled up the support money. She was close. After the spaghetti dinner at the church, she'd probably have enough. I tried to wrap my brain around the fact: She was really going.

My husband and I sat down and looked over the papers we had to send in with the money.

If we signed this, we agreed that they were not liable in the event of her death. I stared at the wording. Death. Heather's death.

My husband signed and handed me the pen. Thoughts of Abraham readying the knife to sacrifice his son Isaac to God's will crossed my mind. Abraham had obeyed.

I signed the paper.

Preparing for the trip consumed our free time. Buying proper clothing included high-top work boots to protect from snakebites, the thought of which nailed my fears firmly to my heart. I busied myself trying to help Heather fit everything into one duffle bag—not an easy task for a teenage girl away from home for seven weeks.

We piled into the car in the wee hours of the morning. I thanked God for the shroud of darkness—Heather didn't need to see my face. I wanted to pull myself together to say good-bye.

Fluorescent lights at the bus terminal cast a surreal haze on the scene. I could barely see through my puffy red eyes and cloudy contacts. I stared at the charter bus ready to take Heather to boot camp in Florida. Young people gathered in clusters with family members. We hugged. I didn't want to let go.

"Mom, I'll be OK."

"I know." I swallowed hard. "I'll miss you."

She hugged her dad and even turned to hug her younger brother before she put her arms around me one more time and squeezed. "I love you, Mom."

In a blink, Heather was on the bus. Her sweet, innocent face smiled from the other side of the window. She made the "I love you" sign she'd learned when we took sign language classes together. She gave us one last wave as the bus pulled out in a great cloud of exhaust.

My husband wrapped his arm around my shoulders. "You did good."

I couldn't talk. My shoulders slumped as my brave façade melted. His eyes told me he felt the same. My son hugged me. "God is in control, Mom," he reminded me.

I knew that, but I didn't feel it. Part of me felt like a zombie. Each day I fought fears. I yearned for my Saturday lunches with Heather, and our bedtime chats. I ached to know what was happening in her life but couldn't even call her.

Ten days passed without a word. Each night we pulled into the driveway and dashed toward the mailbox. Finally, our first letter arrived from her, or maybe I should call it a note. My hands shook as I unfolded the one sheet of boot camp stationery. I treasured every word, even tidbits about floaties in her warm Kool-Aid or the slimy pit she fell into on the obstacle course.

I looked forward to the mail each day, hoping I'd hear something—anything. I missed hearing Heather's voice and her laughter. I gradually let go of my fear and held onto my faith.

We sat around the table eating a late lunch the Sunday before Heather's departure from boot camp for Haiti. "I wonder what she's doing right now," I said.

The phone interrupted.

"It's Heather," my husband said with his hand over the receiver. "Oh, that's wonderful news. . . . I'm so happy to hear that."

My son and I strained to overhear the conversation.

"What?" I leaned closer. "What is she saying?"

Rick handed me the phone. "Here. Talk to her yourself."

"Hi, Heath."

"Hi, Mom. I don't have much time. A lot of other people want to use the phone." Excited chatter filled the background. Heather sounded grown up. I leaned against the wall and cradled the receiver to my ear. Rick and Chris hovered for tidbits of news. Joy and peace that I couldn't explain lifted my spirit. I wanted to stop this moment in time.

"I just wanted you to know I gave my life to the Lord," Heather said. "Dad knows the details."

My spirit soared. I couldn't have asked for more. "I wrote a letter telling you all about it, Mom, but wanted to call now and let you know."

God had answered my prayers! I was at a loss for words. I didn't want to hang up but knew she couldn't hog the pay phone.

"Thanks for calling, Heather. It's so good to hear your voice." I squeezed the receiver. "I love you."

She said a quick hello to her brother and had to go.

I pondered what God had done. I'd prayed for Heather's spiritual growth. He'd answered beyond my dreams. Not only had Heather grown, but God also used the preparation for her trip and boot camp to draw me nearer to him as I learned to trust him with my daughter. Now, she'd head for Haiti.

We sat around the lunch table talking about the wonders of God.

"She's only fourteen," I said. "I wonder what else God has in store."

—Donna Sundblad

THE QUEEN AND THE BOMB

In the grocery store where I shop, I have earned the dubious distinction of being known as the Queen. I was rushing madly through Wilson's Fresh Foods one day, trying to pick up everything before closing time—which is the way I usually do my grocery shopping—when the lights began to flick off and on. A stern-faced clerk walked down the aisles, checking for stray customers; at Wilson's, closing time is swift and systematic.

A girl who looked seventeen, with blond pigtails poking every which way, saw me searching for an open till and waved her arms wildly. "Over here!" she yelled. "I'll put you through!" A few of the staff looked at her and rolled their eyes.

She started checking my groceries, looked me over thoroughly, and said loudly, "You've lost some weight, haven't you? Like a lot."

I plopped my cartons of milk on the conveyer belt and said, "Pardon me?"

Her fingers flew over the cash register keys. "You did. I can tell. That's so cool. You should enter a contest or something. Like Weight Watchers. Don't they have contests? Ever thought about it? You should. I mean it, you could be the queen."

I was mortified; others were obviously listening. Then, in case anyone had missed this bizarre exchange, she crowed, "You've been eating your Special K, baby!"

For some people, age is a sensitive issue. My hot spot is weight. Whether the numbers on the scale go up or down, I don't divulge that information. My weight loss, until this moment, had been a relatively private matter. I wanted to disappear under the candy racks.

"You know what?" she continued, oblivious to my discomfort. "I'll just call you the Queen. You can call me the Bomb. That's what my family calls me because I'm usually out of control. When I get up in the morning, I'm totally miserable, and they say, 'Don't talk to the Bomb—she's not awake yet.'"

She stuffed my groceries into bags. I tried to help so I could escape as quickly as possible. "Come to my register next time," she instructed, cracking her gum.

By this time the lights were out. The clerks impatiently waited for us to finish. "OK," I mumbled and fled.

I learned that her name was Stacey, and whenever she saw me in the store, she would holler, "It's the Queen!"

After my initial embarrassment wore off somewhat, I would dutifully reply, "It's the Bomb!"

From time to time she told me bits of her life. Her parents were divorced. She liked to drink. She had a brown belt in karate and got into fights in bars. She spent part of the time living with her mother, who was strict, and the rest of the time with her father, who let her do whatever she wanted.

A few weeks ago, I went in to pick up some things. She seemed unusually quiet. "What's wrong, Stacey?" I asked.

"I'm tired. I just want to go home," was all she would say. She walked away dejectedly.

Several days later, I needed milk and bread. From halfway across the store I heard, "It's the Queen!" Stacey rushed over. I was in a hurry as usual and mentally reviewed my grocery list as she chattered. But she got my attention when she described how blood had poured from a girl's mouth after Stacey had karate-kicked her in the jaw one night at a bar. "I won't back down from a fight," she declared. "All my friends know that about me. I fight back!"

Somehow, I felt our acquaintance was heading into new territory. The disclosures had deepened. I sensed the Lord wanted me to talk to Stacey about him, but I was in a hurry and other shoppers were detouring around us. We talked briefly about making good choices; it didn't seem like the right time to launch into the gospel. She went back to work, and I went to get the rest of the things on my list, feeling unsettled. It seemed as if I'd missed an opportunity.

However, God was still strolling the aisles of Wilson's: Ten minutes later as I grabbed a bag of frozen corn, Stacey bounced around the corner again, looking for me. "Oh, there you are," she said cheerfully, propping an impossibly high platform shoe on the wheel of my cart.

And so, there in the frozen food section, I sent up a quick prayer, took a deep breath, and told Stacey about the God who loves her, who made her the beautiful, bright young woman she is, who wants the best for her and has a special plan for her life.

She stared at me, amazed. "You're the second person who's told me that!" she exclaimed. "Another girl who works here told me the same thing, and she says she prays for me every day."

How comforting to know that God never sends his

children out alone or unaided. Long before this moment arrived, he had attended to every detail.

"That's not a coincidence, Stacey," I said. "Don't you feel that God is calling your name?"

"I think he's tapping me on the shoulder; sometimes I can actually feel it," she replied dramatically. Then tears filled her eyes, and she said, "You know, I turned bad when my brother committed suicide. He didn't leave a note or anything; no one knows why he did it. That's when I started to fall apart."

Compassion flooded my heart, and suddenly I saw this boisterous, quirky girl as a lost little lamb, stumbling through a fog of confusion and despair while she searched for meaning and significance and peace.

The store was closing, but neither of us went to find a checkout. I talked to Stacey about how my heavenly Father could change her life. She listened, hanging on to every word.

The next morning when I got up, I saw the "instant win" grocery tickets on the kitchen table; in her enthusiasm, Stacey had thrown a bunch of them into my bags. The memory of yesterday's encounter filled me with a stab of joy.

In the frenzied pace of our daily lives, we easily miss doors God has gently pushed ajar, ready to swing open wide at our slightest touch, doors opening into a divine work.

As it turns out, I'm quite happy to be the Queen. This role led me to someone yearning to know the love and hope of our Lord. It's proven to me once again that God delights in turning unlikely situations into awesome opportunities.

—Rachel Wallace-Oberle

BREATHING IN GOD'S PEACE

My world was crashing in around me. My brilliant husband had just taken another hit from multiple sclerosis. John had been diagnosed with MS twenty-six years earlier, when he was only twenty-seven years old. The cruel disease gradually paralyzed him.

Over the first ten years, it had stolen John's ability to walk without support, then to even stand. It continued upward, destroying his ability to sit upright without support. After that, John's arms became useless. Then he began having difficulty speaking and swallowing. MS was like a time bomb ticking endlessly, robbing John of one function after another. When John began having trouble holding his head up, I was afraid of what would go next.

"Oh God, not John's mind," I'd pray. "I depend on that mind."

John had been such a wonderful head of our household: handling the finances, overseeing household repairs, researching the best ways to manage his care. Yet, best of all, John was a wonderful husband and father. Because his disability kept him from working full-time, he poured all he had into guiding our son and me with wisdom and compassion.

John was a highly educated man. No problem existed

that he couldn't find solutions for. Because of his amazing talents, he was asked to be an advocate for the disabled; he even wrote a resource book for people with disabilities. Yet, John lacked one thing—faith in God. Because of this, he was often angry and afraid. His logical mind couldn't grasp the concept of a loving God who would let him continue in failing health, but John longed to believe and even encouraged me to go to church regularly with our son.

"You should go, but it doesn't work for me," John would tell us. "God just doesn't love me."

No one could change John's mind, so he had no access to God's love and peace, which had upheld me through all our struggles, day after day. Yet I also depended on John's mind as a gift from God to give me guidance and wisdom. I felt I would never make it if the MS took his mind away, but that awful day arrived.

Overnight, John's intellect disappeared, leaving him with the mind of a child. And I was left with the heavy load of handling all the things John had done, from managing his complex care to managing the household finances. I'd had enough challenges being John's primary caregiver, raising a son, and keeping a yard and home. Now I had to take over his duties as well! However, my compassionate husband had thoroughly trained me. In fact, John had insisted I learn what needed to be done because he'd been well aware of what MS could do to him. So it wasn't that I didn't know what I needed to do; I just didn't want to face it.

Despite the fact that I was overwhelmed, I knew I needed to join my church group's midweek fellowship. It was good to be in the presence of faith-filled, happy people. Everyone knew what was going on with John. They warmly reached out to me, but I felt numb. My circumstances seemed too much to bear. I felt as if I'd been plunged deeply underwater and was drowning. So, while everyone around me sang praises, I could only croak out a few words before I began to weep. It wasn't that I was mad at God. On the contrary, I was grateful for all the good things he'd done in my life. I tried to lift my hands in appreciation of God's love, but I had no strength. My arms would only tremble. Giving up the struggle, I dropped my hands to my sides. Then the rest of me followed as I dropped first to my knees, then facedown in total surrender to the only One who could help me.

As the praises continued, I whispered, "Jesus, I'm drowning!"

Then I sensed him whisper back, "No, you can breathe here. Breathe!"

So I took a deep breath, then another, and another. My weeping stopped as I concentrated on taking the next breath. I was suddenly aware of my body relaxing. My mind was clearing and absorbing the truths being sung in the praises around me. It was the oddest feeling; I still sensed I was in water over my head, but I was breathing. Remarkably, each breath brought me greater strength and renewed confidence in God. My trembling ceased, my fears were vanishing, and my faith was growing in the power of God to bring us through this trial.

That faith was not in vain. As soon as John's mind became like a little child's, he received Jesus as his Savior and became the most enthusiastic member of our little church. His face was finally free of worry, anger, and doubts about God's love. In fact, John spent his first day as a "new creation" shouting to everyone, "Jesus loves you!" until his voice was gone. He insisted on being baptized that summer. Then, John went to be with his Savior the following spring.

Through it all, I was awed at the patience and the favor of God, who waited for John to understand him. All of John's brilliance, all of his education, all of his kindness to others couldn't get him where God wanted him to go. God loved John so much that he wanted John with him forever. So he tore down that last barrier to John's salvation. Jesus said, "I tell you the truth, unless you turn from your sins and become like little children, you will never get into the Kingdom of Heaven" (Matthew 18:3).

I smile today as I think of my John in heaven with Jesus. And I smile as I think of the grace of our God, who gave him enough time to be a good husband, a good father, and an advocate for the disabled.

Today, as I type, I am using skills John taught me. Our son is now a man who has his father's same wisdom and compassion, yet it's combined with a deep faith due to John's encouragements. And John's book is still for sale on the Internet, guiding the disabled.

The struggles I faced all those years were worth it. Even when the worst happened—the one thing I thought I could never face, the loss of John's brilliance—God was still in control and turned all of it to good.

—Laura L. Bradford

MY MOUNTAIN

"Lord, I can't do this. You know I can't do this." My stomach threatened to toss my half-eaten dinner. Fear tightened around my chest, and tears flowed freely as I thought of what my husband had agreed to do. A week before, I had rededicated my life to God after years of walking a thin line between skepticism and belief. Now God was about to fulfill a desire from my earliest youth.

As a child, I remember sitting on our front lawn looking at the craggy heights of Mt. Hood. Its 11,235 feet rose above the thickly forested carpet of the Oregon Cascade Range. My mother had often told me of her climb to its summit when she was eighteen, and I dreamed of doing the same thing.

In high school I joined the rock-climbing club as a step toward achieving my goal. The first outing was to Beacon Rock, standing tall along the Columbia River. Reaching the top required a steep walk, but no hand-over-hand executions. I set off with the group, laughing and joking, my feet rapidly ascending the path. A quarter of the way up, I slowed, then stopped and backtracked. A barrier blocked the way to realizing my dream of climbing my mountain: I was terrified of heights.

The fear didn't lessen with maturity. On my honeymoon, I tried climbing the stairs to the top of a lighthouse. Halfway up I stopped, then crawled backward to the bottom.

I accepted that I would never stand on Mt. Hood's summit. Yet each time I looked at its majestic peak, the yearning awakened in me and deepened with each year.

Later, I worked part-time at the grade school our three children attended. Two faculty members belonged to Mazamas, a mountaineering club, and I sometimes talked of my longing to climb the mountain. But I never mentioned my fear of heights. When asked why I'd never gone up, I put the blame on my husband, Duane.

"I know he'd never agree, and I wouldn't go without him." This wasn't a total lie. He often said he couldn't understand why anyone would want to climb a mountain. I just knew he'd never do it.

I didn't put my desire before God. I didn't have a daily, close relationship with him at that time. When I was a child, I'd responded to an altar call at a vacation Bible school. But I'd never been discipled or taught the basic tenets of faith, so I'd never grown spiritually. In my late twenties, I even questioned the reality of a Supreme Being and searched for the truth of his existence.

Three years after joining the school faculty, through the patience of our godly principal and several other Christians there, I recommitted my life to God.

A week later a teacher said, "We're putting together a group of novices to climb Mt. Hood, and we want you and Duane to join us. You've always wanted to go up—I'll talk him into it if you have trouble."

I felt caught. I didn't want to explain that I couldn't

make the climb. Then I relaxed. No one talked my strong-willed husband into anything.

Halfway through dinner that night, I told him about the invitation, being sure I could continue to use him as my excuse to decline.

"Let's do it," he said instantly.

I choked on my food, excused myself, and ran to the bedroom. Astonishment rushed through me and threatened to close off my breathing. Whatever made Duane agree to go?

"Lord, how can I get out of this after telling people how much I wanted to climb that mountain? Are you trying to humble me? OK, I'm humbled. But it'll be hard to fess up and tell the truth to everyone."

I reached for my Bible, knowing it contained directions to solving life's dilemmas. With no verses committed to memory, little knowledge of its contents, and no idea of where to start looking, I opened it at random and glanced down. My eyes fell upon these words: "Exalt the LORD our God, and worship at his holy mountain in Jerusalem, for the LORD our God is holy!" (Psalm 99:9).

In disbelief, I read it again, and then I laughed. Was God telling me he would fulfill my dream?

A peace enveloped me. Though some anxiety remained, I knew God would see me through the climb, and I placed myself in his hands. He gave me a verse to take to the summit. "Don't be afraid, for I am with you. Don't be discouraged, for I am your God. I will strengthen you and help you. I will hold you up with my victorious right hand" (Isaiah 41:10).

With a joyful heart, I told everyone we were a go. Duane and I enthusiastically prepared. We learned how to use an ice ax, what to wear, when we would rope together, what to do if someone started to fall, even what food to take. Though already physically fit, we increased our exercise.

Finally, our group of eight greenhorns and two experienced mountaineers began our climb from Mt. Hood's Timberline Lodge at midnight. A full moon and a blanket of stars filled the clear sky. Far in the distance, an orange glow arched over the blackness: the lights from Portland. To the east, we saw the illumination of a smaller town, Madras. Soon the trees began to thin out, and glistening lakes came into view.

We ascended with the sun and the eagles. Many times I felt the cold fingers of fear squeezing my chest. At one place called the chute, we had to use our ice axes and climb hand over hand. Every time terror threatened to overwhelm me, I prayed and recited Isaiah 41:10. God's peace encircled me, a protective shield against panic.

I thought of my mother's climb so many years before. I had all the latest equipment. She'd started way below the timberline, spikes screwed into crepe-soled shoes. I marveled that she'd made it to the top.

When I reached the summit, I looked at the landscape stretched below. I had never been so high above the earth, and the 360-degree view was breathtaking. A plane rising from the Portland airport neared, and I felt I could almost reach out and touch it. This was my dream attained—a loving gift from an adoring Father and a husband who'd climb mountains for me. Praise to God flowed from a grateful heart, and I worshiped at the mountain he'd created.

My stomach still lurches when I look down from heights, but fear no longer controls me. I now climb to places I never could before.

At some point, we all face mountains in life—situations that seem beyond our coping abilities. I've had many to climb—some not much more than hills, others seemingly insurmountable, with lofty peaks. With each new one, I now step out in faith, take God's hand, and trust him. He always takes me to the top.

—**Dori Clark**

CERAMICS 101: PERCHED ON THE MASTER POTTER'S WHEEL

If you want an easy A, take Ceramics 101. Or that was the standard joke on campus. All you had to do was show up in class. Pure and simple.

I can do that! I thought, draped over the tattered arm of the dormitory couch, munching on carrot sticks and studying the next semester's syllabus.

Maybe I could even create a ceramic masterpiece for Mom's birthday, I dreamed. That afternoon, I signed up. This would be the most painless A ever. I almost felt guilty. Almost.

On the first day of class, we craftsman wannabes watched in awe as the instructor flung a slimy gray hunk of clay onto her well-worn potter's wheel. Her feet masterfully went back and forth, spinning the wheel as her hands traveled gracefully upward, her fingers caressing the clay, her thumbs busily forming a center opening, her shoulders swaying to the rhythm of the wheel—virtually a magnum opus unfolding before our very eyes.

Then, voilà! An amazing transformation: That gooey blob had become a tall, stately "vahz." I could not bring myself to call it a vase, it was that stunning.

"Wow! I can do that!" I declared.

Moments later, I stared intently at my own slimy gray

blob, which had been plopped unceremoniously onto my very own potter's wheel. It seemed to stare back, as if to say, "Go ahead. Make my day."

This was obviously going to take a smidgen—OK, a lot—of coordination involving feet, hands, fingers, thumbs, arms, shoulders, even brains (no one had mentioned that in the syllabus). So how could a girl who'd been issued two left ballet slippers at birth and had been mistaken for a one-woman version of Mo, Larry, and Curly pull this off? I was entering uncharted territory, and it would not be a pretty sight.

I patted my hunk-of-clay-with-an-attitude gingerly, hoping we could be friends. Then I threw it firmly onto the center as the instructor had done and started the wheel in motion. Round and round it turned, slowly at first, then faster and faster.

As it gained momentum, a funny thing happened. My hands, cupped around the blob like a miser around his pieces of gold, began to vibrate. Then my elbows joined in, then my shoulders.

Before I knew it, my whole upper torso was in convulsions as my work of art flew off the wheel, soared through the air like a runaway bagel, and landed—*splat!*—across the room.

My further attempts yielded similar results. I was sure other students began to secretly wager where my next flying object would touch down. Every class period was the same: *whomp . . . whirr . . . whe-e-e-e-e!*

Hardly instilling confidence, the instructor seemed to run for cover each time my whirling blob picked up speed on the wheel.

When at last I had miraculously completed a piece that ever so remotely resembled a clay pot, the teacher deemed it unworthy to take up space in the kiln.

My grade? Well, it was not the coveted A I had sought.

"Why?" you ask. "What's so tough about shaping clay on a spinning wheel?"

That's just it! It was the clay. And the wheel. And the spinning. All three. Take away even one of those variables, and I'm certain I'd have been able to present my mom with a beautiful, handmade birthday "vahz" by semester's end.

Without even trying, I managed to achieve a certain level of notoriety that year. Not only was I legendary for my ability to catapult slimy clay into orbit at Mach 2, but equally remarkable was my place in history at the Fine Arts Department of A.S.U. as the first rational being to come out of beginning ceramics with less than an A.

Years later, I came upon a Bible passage in Jeremiah 18 about the potter and the clay and made a startling discovery: I'm somewhat like that clump of clay—gray, mediocre, unwieldy. Yet, in the strong, skilled hands of the Master Potter? Well, I found that I have—we all have—the potential of becoming a vessel for his use and glory.

How does he do it? Ah, there's the rub. The Bible declares that the "wheel" of adversity is one of God's finest tools for molding us into his image. And the "kiln" of affliction is its accomplice. So, when I find myself on his wheel, I'm learning to ask myself some humbling questions:

Am I moldable? Am I willing to yield to his designer plans for me?

Can I endure the fiery furnace as a crucial part of the process?

Do I trust him to make me into a vessel—a valuable masterpiece—for his use?

I want to live in such a way that when the end comes, I will look back and see a life spent eagerly perched on God's wheel, willingly submitting to his transforming touch, patiently enduring the fiery trials of the kiln . . . then joyously fulfilling his purpose for me, for his glory.

We all marveled at our ceramics teacher's ability to take a blob and make a "vahz." How much more do I marvel at our Master Craftsman—amazed, not that he can but that he desires to make a masterpiece of us.

He chooses to take us ordinary clumps of clay—unsightly, unusable, unworthy—do his miracle work in us, and put us to use. An ordinary person in the creative hands of an extraordinary Designer—who can imagine the potential!

"Lord, I think of those times when I, too, stubbornly catapulted myself into parts unknown and landed—*splat!*—in the most unlikely places at the most inopportune times, and you patiently picked me up, dusted me off, and set me lovingly back onto your wheel . . . and, well, I just want to say . . . thanks."

—Sandra Glahn

CLEAR AS A BANNER ON A BEACH PLANE

I walked into the Rite Aid drugstore in search of some toothpaste. I was in Wildwood, New Jersey, with a team of high school and college kids who were determined to evangelize the world. We had all just been given summer jobs in a food-supply establishment. The company liked to hire us "church kids." They said we were honest and put in a hard day's work. The pay wasn't bad, either. And the ocean town was crammed with students looking for any kind of job they could get. I was grateful I already had one.

As I rummaged through the deodorant and shaving cream section, a man with a red Rite Aid Drug smock approached me. He said, "You don't want a job, do you?"

I looked up. He seemed friendly. And a little desperate. In a way, I wanted to help him. But I already had a job, as did all the others in our group. So I said, "No, sorry. But if I hear of someone needing one, I'll let them know you're looking."

He thanked me.

That Monday, I started my new job in the butcher shop. At first it was interesting—all those cow rib cages hanging in the food locker. Grinding up hundred-pound boxes of frozen Australian beef was different, if somewhat unexciting. Even though it left a lingering smell of death in the air, I didn't think it was that bad.

I didn't think it was that bad for about two hours, anyway. Then, going in and out of the freezers and back to the hot air of the shop left me with a headache. I felt nauseated. After a whole day of it, I went home feeling depressed. All the other kids seemed very happy with their jobs. But I wondered, *Can I take a whole summer of this?*

However, I didn't feel good about the possibility of quitting already. Weren't we Christians? Didn't Christians put in a "hard day's work"? Weren't we "honest"?

But did that mean I had to feel like throwing up every minute I was at work?

I gritted my teeth and hoped it would get better.

After two more days, I was on the brink of despair. How could I make it through a whole summer of this?

I thought of that job at the Rite Aid store, but I figured by now it was gone. "That was three days ago," I mumbled.

But then it occurred to me—Why did God let that guy even ask me? Maybe he knew I'd get sick on this one.

That seemed logical. Proverbs 3:5-6 came to mind: "Trust in the LORD with all your heart; do not depend on your own understanding. Seek his will in all you do, and he will show you which path to take."

I prayed, "Lord, if you want me to take that job, then let it still be available. For some reason, you made me aware of it. And I know I can't stand this butcher shop."

I decided to go for it and sped off to the drugstore.

The job was still available. In fact, the manager asked me if I knew of two more people who needed something. I went back to our summer house and told everyone at dinner. Two others, Dan and Jane, were interested, and when we went over, all three of us were hired.

We got a schedule and began working, stocking the shelves and keeping busy in the store. It was a decent job with decent pay, and I had no complaints. In fact, I was amazed to see how God had worked. Proverbs 3:6 says, "He will show you which path to take." So I figured that Scripture was right on.

Then one morning several weeks later, after we all arrived to start the day, our boss called us into the back office. He told us he had to let all three of us go. "We made a mistake and overestimated how much help we'd need. I'm sorry."

Both Jane and Dan were visibly upset. They'd never been "let go" before. When we got outside, Dan said, "We were just fired."

I said, "'Laid off' sounds better."

"I don't care how you put it. It's the same thing. We can't collect unemployment insurance."

Jane was more realistic. "We've got a bigger problem, guys. It's halfway through the summer, and there's no chance of getting a job now. What are we going to do?"

We stopped and prayed, but I could see the fear on both their faces. "I've got to get enough money for my second year in college," Dan said.

Jane agreed. "Let's go back to the butcher shop."

They went back that very morning and had jobs immediately. But there was no way I was going back to that butcher shop. What to do?

It was nice not having to go to work. But I was going to school that fall, too, and needed tuition money. I had to get a job, quick. Where could I start? The want ads were sparse, and any jobs offered were mostly dishwashing, hauling garbage, or stock work. The manager at Rite Aid had specifically told me, "Mark, never go into stock work. You're not very good at it."

I asked him why. He replied, "You spend too much time being friendly with the customers. You should learn to just tell them what they want and get on with it."

I felt a little glum and figured I should try something else. But what? Again, Proverbs hit me. "Trust in the LORD with all your heart."

Right. But was he going to produce another job?

I went to the beach in the afternoon and lay on my towel, praying and hoping that God would show me something, as he had before.

I watched the gulls dip and peck at discarded food on the beach. I listened to the breakers and the cries of children. I heard in the distance the buzz of one of the single-prop planes that went by all day with long banners on the back, advertising some company in town. I read the signs as they went by, whipping in the wind. There was one about a restaurant I knew of. Then another about one of the piers on the boardwalk with rides and games.

A third one came popping along with an even longer banner. I watched it flap in the breeze. It said, "Wildwood Lumber Company." Nothing too spectacular. But at the end was a huge happy face in yellow.

Suddenly, I sat upright. Below the happy face was written "Jesus Loves You." It was the first time I'd ever seen such a thing in Wildwood. Until that moment, I figured it was a major center of hedonism and pagan fun. But then it occurred to me, *Maybe they would offer me a job.*

I got up, went home, and looked up the address in the phone book. I borrowed a bike and rode down to the huge lumber center in the middle of town.

Once inside, I asked for the owner and asked him if he was responsible for the inscription on the banner. "I am," he said. He was a slim, balding guy with a wide smile.

I decided to be blunt. "Are you a Christian?"

"Yes." He smiled. "Are you?"

I told him about my conversion, now over a year ago, and how I was working in a local ministry for the summer. Then I told him I needed a job.

His face clouded. "I don't know. We don't really need anyone right now." But he appeared to be thinking. Then he said, "Wait a second. Maybe we could use you."

He took me back in the building and showed me some furniture that needed to be put together. "Can you do that?"

"Definitely."

He hired me. I stayed the whole summer. It was good not only to work for a Christian but also to know that God got personally involved with my job search. One thing is sure: When God answers, he makes it as clear as a banner on a beach plane!

—Mark R. Littleton

A LITTLE BIT OF PARADISE

I woke to the feel of crisp sheets, the hum of air conditioning, and that tingly afterglow on my skin from a little too much sun the day before. I smiled contentedly. I was in Mexico with my husband. The room had that wonderful enveloping darkness that only hotels have, where one could sleep all day with no idea the world was moving on.

I tiptoed on cool tiles to our balcony. The tropical, humid morning settled on me like a warm blanket. Spread before me was a little taste of paradise. The hazy ocean expanded out to the horizon and beyond with the distant moaning of a ship. The sounds of the rhythmic rising and falling of ocean waves washed up to me.

I leaned over the balcony and looked below. Hotel staff in starched white uniforms primped the grounds like a woman preparing for a date—pruning here, clipping there, trimming bushes, and sweeping walks. Carts rumbled by with trays of food, glasses, and towels. A man gracefully swept a net back and forth through an absurdly blue and incredibly sculpted pool, catching every stray limb and leaf. He was surrounded by rows of white lounge chairs waiting for their guests. A slight breeze swayed the palm trees and carried just the briefest whiff of breakfast.

I faced a delicious day of nothing. Lazy nothing. Warm nothing. Completely relaxed nothing. Our biggest decision was where to deposit our bodies for the day. Should we choose the lounge chairs next to the pool with the waterfall, or should we start out at the beach?

Still, despite the lovely laziness, I had to acknowledge that I felt a nagging disappointment in my spirit. I had prayed before the trip and each morning of the trip that God would use me to minister to someone in some way. I had no idea what form that would take, but I had prayed for an opportunity to love someone in a way I knew that only God could orchestrate.

But no "God moment" had materialized, and now it was our last day in Mexico.

Did I miss something, Lord? I asked.

We showered and dressed, then meandered toward the enticing aroma of breakfast. People in bright vacation clothes nodded and smiled as we passed. As we walked down the hall, we heard the clink of juice glasses and the murmur of voices. Then we turned the corner to behold an expansive array of food. Guests walked by with plates overflowing. Bowls of fresh fruits—mangos, papayas, kiwis, and strawberries—were nestled amid ice and decorative red and orange hibiscus blooms. Heat lamps spotlighted trays of bacon, sausages, and various entrées. Shrimp and salmon were fanned out on chilled plates surrounded by cheeses. A rainbow of juice glasses sparkled at one end of the buffet. *This must be what the feasts in heaven are like,* I thought.

We sat out on the veranda and savored our breakfast. Comfortable under the slowly turning fans, we held hands, lingered over our coffee, chatted, laughed, and planned our day—to bask in the sun with books and cool drinks.

We wandered out through the hotel grounds and ended up in lounge chairs by the waterfall.

As we surrendered ourselves to our lazy day, the sun started its stroll across the sky. I closed my eyes and listened to the water, the murmur of voices, and the cadence of tropical birds. Hours rolled by without my even realizing it. The afternoon settled on us, and I pulled out my Bible study. I paused and looked around me. *Oh Lord,* I thought, *this is beautiful. You are such a creative God. Thank you for the gift of this vacation.*

I mused about the massage I had scheduled for later that day and smiled. The sounds all around me blurred together as I entered the Lord's presence. Almost like a whisper in the wind or a voice in my spirit, I felt the Lord ask me to give up my massage and give that money to someone who obviously needed it more than I did.

I silently dismissed the thought and tried to continue my Bible study. But as if he were behind me tapping me on the shoulder, God continued to ask. Verses I read seemed to reiterate that message, and I couldn't dismiss the nagging thought.

OK, Lord, I'll do it, I decided. But even as I agreed, I started to have my doubts. *How will I know who to give it to? Everyone here could use it.*

We were going to the market later to buy gifts, and I decided that is where I would give the money away.

Lord, you have to make it very clear to me who I should give it to. I'll be distracted with shopping, so please get my attention, I prayed.

We showered and dressed and headed to the market. Barefoot children with big brown eyes held up trinkets for sale. Food stands lined the street with homemade tortillas, burritos, and mangos artistically sculpted on sticks. The market was a brightly colored maze of booths displaying silver jewelry, bright fabrics, hand-painted bowls and dishes. We wandered through the offerings, listening to nearby Mexican guitar music.

We passed a booth where a tired young mother in an embroidered pink dress sat on a stool, helping her son with his homework. We continued weaving through the market, and I suddenly realized that I was supposed to give my money to that woman.

We knew it would be tricky to find our way back to the woman, so we worked our way up and down each aisle. As we turned a corner, I spotted her. Then I realized I had no idea what I would say, and my heart started to pound. *What if I was wrong? How do I really know this is the person I'm supposed to give the money to?*

I walked up to the woman, bent down with the money in my hand, and said, "I want to give you this money."

She stood up, noticed I didn't have any wares in my hand, and said, "What do you buy?"

"I don't want to buy anything. I just want to give you this money," I said. She looked confused.

What now? I thought.

Her husband walked up and asked, "Can I help you?"

"I would like to give you this money," I said, holding up the bills.

"What would you like to buy?" he asked and turned toward his booth.

I shook my head. "I don't want to buy anything. I would like to give you this money."

"But why?" he asked.

They were staring at me. My heart was still pounding.

"Well, I just felt like God told me to give it to you," I stammered.

He started to cry. "Oh thank you, thank you, ma'am. It is the end of the month, and we didn't know how we were going to pay our rent! Oh, thank you, thank you!"

He quickly explained to his wife in Spanish, gesturing toward me. She put her hand over her mouth and tears came to her eyes.

I was overcome with emotion as he took my hands and looked into my eyes with sincere gratitude. He exclaimed, "Thank you, thank you so much!"

I started to cry through my smile, "You are so welcome!"

He kept calling out to me as we walked away, "Thank you, thank you."

God had so clearly stepped into my world and orchestrated a very detailed plan that I was privileged to be part of, and I was so humbled. I guess I was just as much in awe of the fact that I had actually heard his voice as I was that I had obeyed him.

The Lord knew months and years before we ever planned this trip what would take place. He penned the date we would go, out of all the dates we could have chosen. He knew this family would need this money on that day and that I would listen and obey. He scheduled the hour we'd walk through the market. All the exact timing and details of God's plan awed me. He loved that family that much. He loves me that much. He loves you that much. Stunning! Now this is a little bit of paradise!

—Tamara Vermeer

SERVING UP ANSWERS TO OUR NEEDS

Most days when my grandson, John, got home from his after-school job, he would dash from the front door to the refrigerator in two giant steps. And when I got home from work, he would already be building a fire in the fireplace while his snack heated in the microwave.

But one day after Christmas vacation, I came in the back door just as John, a high school freshman, shuffled in the front door. He made no attempt to remove his band jacket, dropped his backpack to the floor, and sprawled on the couch.

His scowl was ominous, but the only explanation from him was a long, deep sigh.

"Hi, John. How was your day?" Grandmothering 101 had taught me that nonchalance was the best tool for conversing with teenagers.

Another excruciating sigh answered my question. Grandmothering 101 had also explained that second sighs indicated a serious money concern.

As John slouched on the couch, continuing to sigh, I pulled out my greatest weapon. I remember wondering, *Why is prayer my last resort when it should be my only response?*

Heading to the kitchen, begging God for help, I thought I heard him whisper, "I understand—I've parented you a long time. You keep forgetting that I care even about the lilies," he added, referring to Matthew 6:30.

I took hot chocolate to the living room. John accepted the warm nourishment but kept scowling.

"OK, Tiger. What's up?" I asked, direct and to the point.

"I can't take Carol Ann to the winter formal. My part-time job doesn't pay enough for a stupid dance. To go to the dance, you gotta get a limousine and have dinner at The Nest. Grandma, do you have *any* idea how much it costs to eat at a place like that? Then I have to buy the dance tickets, and Andrew said somethin' about corsages!"

"I see. You have a big price tag there. Can you give me a few days to think about it?" I said.

John rolled his eyes and mumbled, "I guess I have to. That means we'll pray about it, but I don't know where God will get that much money!"

Little did John know how many things God would have to work out for him during the next seventy or eighty years, and today I had no idea how to fix this problem. At age fifteen, John was holding down a part-time job, and out of a meager paycheck, he saved some, gave some to God, and paid for extra, fun stuff. Still, I wasn't comfortable just handing over money for one evening's entertainment. During the next few days, I stewed about the dance, about money, and about teen-agers in general, and I prayed.

I went about my business as usual, but my mind kept reflecting on my own "good old days." I came of age in the 1950s when "proper" young ladies wore hats, high heeled shoes, and gloves to church and when formal affairs demanded long evening gowns and elbow-length gloves.

Then, even while a plan began forming in my mind,

I remembered how God had shown his care about *my* everyday life. Through the years, I had leaned heavily on God as I walked a fragile line between the two loves of my life: my disabled daughter, Anne, and her son, John. I was the breadwinner, rule maker, detention officer, and female head of our fatherless household, while my daughter was John's mother. My job was to teach him to respect, honor, and love her while obeying me.

I prayed for courage because my plan would tamper with icons of the modern teenage world. At supper that night, I spoke.

"You know, John, I could serve a formal dinner for four at home before the dance. Your mom could help. It might be fun, and . . . "

Before I finished my rehearsed sales pitch, John grinned. "Wow! Would you really do that?"

"Sure, if you can make it OK with the other three." He was already on the way to the telephone.

His date, Carol Ann, said, "It's OK with me if Ashley agrees."

Ashley said, "Fine with me if it's OK with my date, Austin."

Shocked that teens would step outside the box so easily, I turned to my faithful old friend, the *Betty Crocker Cookbook,* for a menu that did not include pizza.

Oh dear! My kitchen/dining room could be a roadblock. John's buddies hung out at our house, knowing I would whip up bunkhouse grits at the drop of a cowbell. They gobbled everything set before them on my large, round dining table, which was at one end of our oversized country kitchen and with a full view of the kitchen sink. A formal dinner in the kitchen, with girls, was not appropriate for the evening I had in mind.

Setting aside my pride, I made a few phone calls. Sure enough, one gracious friend offered the use of his country home, complete with a formal dining room, and he insisted on serving as the chauffeur for the unlicensed teens.

On the appointed night, Lenox china gleamed on a white linen tablecloth, stemmed glassware sparkled in soft candlelight, and strains of "Clair de Lune" warmed the elegant dining room. Just as the clock chimed seven, my friend drove his Lincoln Town Car into his driveway and deposited the young guests at the front door. As the tantalizing aroma of rosemary chicken drifted from the kitchen, I welcomed our guests, whose faces resembled those of anxious five-year-olds on the first day of kindergarten. The opening phase of my grandson's first high school winter formal was under way.

John's mom ushered the guests into the formal living room, where we served tomato-juice cocktails and assorted hors d'oeuvres. The boys seemed stiff in their suits and ties and sat on the edge of the couch. The girls were beautiful in glittering long gowns but had obviously worn high heels only to church. On the other hand, my daughter and I presented calm, professional exteriors in black slacks, white shirts, and red-and-white-striped aprons for our roles as chief cook, maître d', servers—and dish washers.

When I announced, "Dinner is served," the young men escorted their ladies to the candlelit dining room, mumbling about reading name cards in the dark. A salad and water goblet waited at each place, so after John, as the host, offered a blessing, I poured iced tea, set a small dinner bell at my grandson's right hand, closed the dining room door, and retired to the kitchen to dish up the entrée.

Shortly, we realized that leaving the dinner bell with the "host" was a huge mistake. John gleefully rang that bell all evening. He kept his mom and me busy scurrying back and forth refilling glasses of tea, replacing dropped forks, and finding lost napkins. I smiled through clenched teeth as he rang that bell over and over. He was in his element, summoning servants while reigning at the head of the table with elegant charm.

Uttering a quick prayer, I finally assembled the dessert. I placed a delicate scoop of French vanilla ice cream on each piece of my prize brownies, then carefully drizzled chocolate syrup on top of the ice cream in an artsy design. A light dusting of powdered sugar completed each confection.

After dinner, the boys-turned-gentlemen assisted the young ladies into their formal wraps, leaving wrist corsages intact. Each of them thanked me profusely. My friend drove our guests to the dance, where they finally became the responsibility of other parents, teachers, and chaperones.

With mixed emotions, I cleaned the kitchen, loaded my pots and pans into my car, thanked my friend for the use of his lovely home, and sincerely thanked God the evening was over.

I aged significantly that evening, but a couple of years later, John asked for a repeat performance for his senior—and final—winter formal affair. He remembered to tell me there would be eight guests and that Ashley would be his date.

Knowing for a fact that God truly cares about our everyday lives as well as our formal dinners, I said, "Sure, we can do that."

However, I *did* forget to supply a dinner bell.

—Liz Hoyt Eberle

PRISON TEACHER

"I've found just the job for you," Jack said, as he entered the door of our apartment. "If you agree, we can set up an interview appointment."

He stood with his overcoat over his arm, giving me a look of challenge. I realized there would be something different about this job.

I was thirty-two years old, he was forty, and we'd been married for one week. We were much in love; but neither of us had been married before, and we didn't know everything about each other yet. Jack was not sure if I would accept this opportunity, although he knew how much I wanted to teach. He opened the closet door and put away his overcoat. Then, he sat beside me on the sofa and began to explain.

The nearby federal prison was expanding its education program. Previously, the instruction had covered the equivalent of high school; now, the administrators wanted someone who could give courses in composition and literature on the beginning college level. The prison staff had turned to the college where Jack taught physics to ask if anyone with the necessary credentials was available.

I had a master's degree in comparative literature and had taught freshman English at a state university.

"That's a men's prison!" I objected. "Would they hire a woman?"

"They might. This is a young men's prison, for guys who are past the legal age to be treated as juveniles. Eighteen to twenty-five—just about the age level you've taught. They are mostly first offenders, not murderers, not lifers. The closest thing to violent types would be the bank robbers."

Jack regarded me closely.

With different feelings surging inside me—*I may be teaching!* versus *Am I really up to this?*—I said, "Let's set up the interview!" My voice shook only a little.

"Why do you want to teach a bunch of crooks?" the interviewer asked me after we had discussed my credentials and experience.

He leaned back in his swivel chair, giving me a steady look much like the one Jack had given when he first told me.

Should I say, "Because I heard there was an opening"? That seemed too brutally honest. I tried another kind of honesty. "It's a matter of degree, isn't it? I have taught plagiarists, draft dodgers, and just plain amoral people. Most of us have, at some time, done something we are not proud of. These men have done something worse than most of us have done. They got caught, and they are being punished for it."

It must have been the right answer. I got the job.

My students represented many races and ethnic groups. Of course, I knew that, unlike the university freshman class, these would be all young men who wore the same clothes and had the same haircut. But there was another difference from the college students: Never once did a student say, "But I can't think of anything to write about!"

They always had something to write about! It might be

self-centered or angry. It might be extreme (there were both radicals and reactionaries) or it might not. They wrote themes in the form of fiction or nonfiction, long or short, some good enough to be published, some barely literate. One of my students went from total illiteracy to high school equivalent in a year and a half. He was uneducated but clearly had never been stupid!

Whatever the range of style or ability, everyone had something to say.

Class discussions, as often happens in literature or composition courses, covered a wide range of subjects. The question of my own religious faith came up. I warned them that I had to be careful of what I said: "After all, I am teaching in a public institution!" I got a friendly laugh for that, and one student called out, "No one will tell on you!" I shared my Christian perspective.

One man, Nathan, gave me a letter he had written to his ex-girlfriend. He wanted to know if he should send it or not. It began with his detailed reminiscences of their romance. It followed with a frank confession of everything he had done wrong in their relationship. It ended with a complete, genuine acceptance of her decision to marry someone else.

The letter almost made me cry. I felt a great deal of responsibility for being entrusted with it. Writing it had been good therapy for Nathan, and I was glad that he had. But I realized that because he was willing to let her go, it might be best not to send it.

Previously, I had read a psychological study on the effects of grief in the recovery of burn patients after a fire at an apartment complex. Some guidelines of healthy and unhealthy grief had been developed from this. I used Nathan's letter (with his permission) as the basis for a class lecture on using experiences as a basis for writing, with focus on the experience of loss and grieving. Grieving was a part of these men's lives. Some were being divorced and their children raised never to know them. Some had parents that never visited.

As I gave the lecture on writing as a way of working through their grief and loss, an intense silence filled the class, and every eye was riveted in my direction. I knew the students were connecting with my topic in very personal ways.

At the end of the class period, students left, mostly in silence, with just friendly nods to me or a whispered "Thanks." However, Nathan lingered. He had seen that his letter precisely followed the stages of grief; he saw that there was no need to send it. The letter had already served its true purpose: to further Nathan's healing.

It would be beside the point to say that these men "deserved" the pain of their losses. That was exactly what made it so hard.

One of the most articulate students explained his experience: He had been in the marines before he became a criminal. In some ways being in the marines was the same as being in prison. In the marines he had to wear a uniform and had very little choice about how to spend his time or even what he ate or when he slept, just as in prison. If anything, being in the marines was more demanding.

Yet in the marines, he was proud. In prison, it was punishment. What was the difference? The guilt.

Many of my students had been involved with intoxicating drink or drugs, although that might not have been the specific charge on the record. Other prison workers told me that these "sick" ones could be the hardest to rehabilitate. The bank robbers, on the other hand, just needed a strong, selfish reason to "go straight," and they frequently did.

But the most tragic incident of the year involved a bank robber. I was in the prison lobby, waiting for the inner gate to be unlocked so I could go to my class. As usual, I had lifted the handset of the internal telephone to report in.

Suddenly I heard a flurry of voices, rushing footsteps, a siren, and the crack of a rifle outside. I was facing the lobby window and could see, framed against the dark of that February evening, the red streak of a bullet—something I had never seen before.

"Get off the phone, get off the phone," shouted the man at the desk. I had frozen, with the handset in my hand, unable to think. I hung up. I heard him say, "Ambulance!"

As I stood, petrified and very much aware that I was in a prison, a dangerous place, a prison worker came inside with blood on his hands and face; he had been trying to give mouth-to-mouth resuscitation to the would-be escapee, but it was useless.

I heard masculine sobs from a nearby room—sobs of someone who didn't care who heard. I found out later that one of the dead man's buddies had helped him attempt this escape. We had no classes that evening—the prison was in lockdown. Just as we teachers and other outside staff were leaving, I overheard someone say, "Record one man released to death."

The grimness of that statement left me shaken. I was glad to get back to my apartment and to Jack's arms.

The buddy who had assisted the escape attempt was transferred to Leavenworth maximum security penitentiary.

Neither the dead man nor his too-helpful buddy was in my class, but some of my students knew one or both of them. When class resumed, they wanted to write or talk only about the escape attempt. For the first time, I was stern with my class. "Don't any one of you do nonsense like that! Somebody cares about you!" They nodded solemnly.

In some ways, my students reminded me of children. They would play tricks on me. Three of them were short, stout, blond men, and it was easy for me to get confused. They would sit together and answer to each other's names when I took the roll. After a while, I would just glance up and say, "Smith, Jones, and Green are all here," then go on to the rest of the names.

Ironically, near the end of that year—the year I had taught the relationship of grief and writing—Jack died. We had been married only fourteen months. My students sent me a condolence card they'd all signed. The first three names were Smith, Jones, and Green. I could imagine the three of them jostling to be first in line, and in that exact order. They knew I would see the message: We are all still here.

I have gone on to other teaching jobs, and I now have a different husband. But I learned more from my students that year than I have in many other years. Perhaps the lesson that has stayed with me the most is the importance of just knowing that someone cares.

—Lucy Michaels

THE RIGHT DECISION

"Daddy car now?"

I gently led Madi from the church nursery. We were alone today because it was my wife's shift at the hospital, but I didn't mind. Our father-daughter weekends were special, and I enjoyed picking Madi up from the nursery almost more than I enjoyed the service. Her joyful squeals at seeing me gave our studies in Galatians stiff competition.

"We're going," I replied, carefully navigating through the crowd. "We need our coats first, though."

"Get coats an' play wit' rock!"

I chuckled. Next to the coats, a polished stone roughly the size of a shoe propped open the church office door. Ever since Madi started carrying things, the stone had become her holy grail. She wasn't quite strong enough to lift it, but for now she contented herself with grabbing the stone, grunting futilely while exclaiming with girlish glee, "It too 'eavy!"

We were heading toward the coats when one word turned my head.

"Kevin?"

I saw a woman with short brown hair, holding a girl slightly younger than Madi. Though years had weathered her face, her eyes sparked recognition. Suddenly everything faded as I remembered a long-forgotten moment years before.

"Kevin?" she had said in that same voice. . . .

It was no wonder I hadn't heard her back then. I had been more concerned with unloading the heavy pallet I lugged, then climbing into my beat-up car, getting home without falling asleep at the wheel, and dining on takeout alone in my apartment for my twenty-seventh birthday. The main festivity would be watching *The Late Show,* but after that I'd go straight to bed because I needed to awaken early the next day for my other full-time job as an aide at a local elementary school. I'd blown my chance at teaching, so now I had to be content with watching others do what I loved while I was their errand boy. My life was tainted by the delusion that fate hadn't been kind, but actually, I had no one to blame but myself. God had blessed me, but I'd squandered it, so there I was—stocking freight second shift at Wal-Mart by night and corralling autistic students during the day.

"Kevin?" she had said again all those years ago. "Don't tell me you don't remember me. I stalked you all over Sears four years ago just to get your phone number."

Well, that pierced my self-pity. I skidded to a stop and braced the hand truck behind me, slowing the steadily rolling pallet full of housewares. I glanced over to the toys and spied a familiar vision of beauty.

Susie Engstrom. My heart skipped double time, my face flushed, and I'm pretty sure I grinned like a fool. Susie and I had worked at Sears before this, during our college years—she was upstairs in the clothing department while I was down in hardware.

"Stalked" was an exaggeration. She'd actually sauntered in front of the hardware department for days, casting seductive glances over her shoulder, the kind of come-on that made even grandfatherly priests go weak in the knees. Not being grandfatherly nor a priest, I'd hardly been immune to her charms.

We'd never furthered our attraction—just skirted around it for a few weeks until she quit Sears. I hadn't seen her again.

Now, here she was at Wal-Mart, as beautiful as the last time I'd seen her. Her full figure was eye catching, her long brown hair was lustrous, and her skin still glowed with a golden-brown tan.

On this birthday—a night I'd expected to spend alone—running into Susie was an unexpected boon. I'd heard that she was married, but that hadn't seemed to hinder her interest in me.

I'd tanked my first and only teaching position at a Christian school because I cared more about my selfish desires than serving God and was now restraining slightly dangerous autistic children for barely above minimum wage. I'd bombed out of graduate school, leaving my academic career in ruins. I was in debt up to my eyeballs, so much so that I didn't answer the phone anymore for fear creditors would be on the line.

Good choices had not been high on my list of priorities, so with desperate enthusiasm I grinned and managed, "Hey, Susie. How're things?"

Her responsive smile was all the encouragement I needed. Married or not, Susie was glad to see me, and a peculiar mix of excitement and familiar dread filled me—excitement, because I was tired of coming home to an answering machine whose little red light never blinked; dread, because deep inside I sensed bad choice number 537 just around the corner.

She smiled warmly, and a sudden headiness made me woozy. "I'm all right, I suppose," she answered, leaning in slightly, her posture suggesting she was significantly more "all right" because I was there. "I'm working part-time at Hallmark and taking classes at college."

"Really? What classes?"

She tilted her head slightly, and there was something in those eyes—a spark of desire inconsistent with someone who was happily married. "Early childhood education," she whispered huskily.

I nodded, not really caring but asking anyway because decorum demanded it, "How's married life? Treating you well?"

Her eyes dimmed, shadowed by real pain. Some of her excitement faded as she replied softly, "No, actually . . ." She sighed and continued, "Brad and I had problems and just kept fighting. We got divorced last spring."

Part of me was tap dancing right about then. However, I was still partly human, so I offered genuine sympathy—not feeling all that bad for Brad, however. "Man, Susie. I am sorry."

She shrugged gallantly. "I'm working things out. That's why I'm back in college, trying to do it over . . . getting a new life."

She looked at me intently after the words "new life" and asked, "So, how are you?"

I wanted to say, "Great! I'm doing well—just taking a break from school to pay off some debts." I couldn't, though.

Truthfully, I was lost. I'd tried to live my way, but I'd

botched everything. I'd made my own choices, but they'd led only to a slummy apartment, dead-end jobs, overwhelming debt, and shameful impurity.

A tempting thought arose, countering my depression and self-pity: *Get her number; ask her out. You don't have to be alone.*

It sounded logical. Susie obviously wanted that; it was in her eyes, clear as day, and hey, she was divorced. Whatever happened, no one would get hurt because she was alone.

Like me.

Bad choice number 537 loomed large in her dark brown eyes, but who cared? No one.

Except me.

Well, only a little, and only lately. I'd been reading my Bible some, but I was amazed at how much quieter I was inside. Things weren't wonderful, but they weren't terrible, either.

It struck me just then: I didn't really need Susie. I wanted her . . . but I didn't need her. She wasn't what my heart hungered after.

However, how bad a choice could she be? Didn't I owe myself some fun?

Then I remembered something Susie's stunning, sensory-overloading presence had almost erased, but there it was, working through my mind like a persistent sliver.

My sister had called the previous week with a scheme to set me up on a date. Apparently, she and a friend had decided to play matchmaker for their respective older siblings; they were worried we'd never meet "the one" because we'd stopped trying.

The girl was a Christian—as I was, as I'd repeatedly told Susie I was, though I'd given her plenty of reasons four years previous to disbelieve my claim.

Now, Susie was here at Wal-Mart—extremely attractive, as lonely and hurting as I was, certainly willing—and the date my sister had arranged, a girl named Abby I didn't even know, was not.

I remember I licked dry lips and said, "Things are good, I guess. I'm working double shifts to pay off a little debt . . ."

We chatted about mundane trivialities for a few moments, and then I said, "Listen, it was great chatting, but I gotta get back to work." I threw a thumb unconvincingly over my shoulder at the pallet behind me. "If I don't get this on the shelves before midnight, I'll get busted big-time."

She nodded, the light fading from her eyes. "Sure, no problem." She stepped away, lingering slightly as she said, "Take care, Kevin."

I nodded, lugging my pallet and its wares away. Though I saw genuine disappointment in her eyes and felt a little bad about that, each step away from her flooded me with a relief I'd never known before.

That weekend, I met my wife, Abby, at her church. We had lunch, saw a movie, and never looked back. . . .

Now, years later at church, my eyes refocused on Susie—older, still good-looking, but nothing like the beauty I'd run into again at Wal-Mart fifteen years ago. For a moment, I was slightly nervous and then realized with relief that I felt . . . nothing.

I smiled and asked, "Susie Engstrom?"

She smiled also, but not the enticing grin I remembered. "No, it's still Seely. Brad and I remarried three years ago." She paused, adding, "We got saved not long after that."

Once again, I was grinning like a fool . . . for an entirely different reason. "Susie, that's great."

Eyes shining, she replied, "Isn't it, though?" She hoisted the little girl in her arms, saying softly, "This is Katy."

I nodded, saying, "And this is Madison," even though my daughter was more interested in her beloved rock by the coatracks than meeting an old friend.

"So what are you up to these days?" she asked, friendly interest the only thing I saw in her eyes.

"Well, I've been teaching junior high English for six years," I answered, those words still sounding great to my ears, "and I was just accepted into Binghamton University's Creative Writing Master's Program."

She smiled. "That's great." She nodded at Madi, smiling even wider. "Is she your only one?"

"Nope," I replied cheerily, "we've got number two coming in four months."

Susie fairly beamed. "Wow," she whispered, laying a hand on my forearm, and I still felt nothing. "God is good, isn't he?"

I nodded, my neck feeling like a gigantic bobble-head. "He certainly is."

"Daddy?"

I looked down at Madi, who stared up at me, cherubic face framed by golden curls, eyes blinking owlishly behind petite glasses. "What's up, pumpkin?"

"Wanna play wit' rock!"

"In a minute, kiddo. Listen," I said to Susie, holding my anxious two-year-old at bay, "I don't mean to be rude, but how did . . ." I trailed off, the obvious question left unsaid.

Her face softened, but her countenance still beamed. "It

was that night, at Wal-Mart. You walked away from me, even when you knew I didn't want you to. That must have been hard." She paused, glancing lovingly at Katy. "You always used to talk about being a Christian, and until that night, I always thought you were blowing smoke. Walking away like that, despite what we both wanted . . . made me look into the whole Christian thing." She looked back at me, gracing me with the smile of a mother and a loving, faithful wife. "And here I am."

I smiled. "Here you are, indeed."

We chatted about trivialities and then went our separate ways, I marveling about our choices and how God protects us from ourselves until we finally make the right one.

—Kevin Lucia

DRY GROUND

I had no idea that while I was shopping with my two oldest daughters, our basement family room had begun filling with water. Days of steady rain had caused area rivers to overflow their banks, but I wasn't really concerned about it because our house was built on a high hill. However, as the three of us tried on shoes, water was pooling around the legs of our new sofa.

Rain was coming down hard when I pulled the car into our driveway. Yelling and giggling, the three of us dashed into the house. I was the first one through the door, and what I saw took me several seconds to comprehend. Our front room was crowded with boxes, toys, books, and games that normally would have been in our finished basement. My daughters tried to squeeze around me. When they saw the jumble of chairs and the antique trunk that belonged downstairs, their laughter died.

I dropped my bag on the floor and ran for the basement stairs, crying to the girls, "We've got water!"

Near the bottom of the stairs, I stopped and stared. The lovely cream carpet was three inches under water. Old coffee cans from the garage were stacked under each leg of the sofa and loveseat, raising the furniture out of harm's way. The heavy television stand and computer table already showed damage as the wood absorbed the water. I watched my husband furiously running our Shop-Vac, the machine's roar echoing off the walls as it pulled liquid into the tank. When his eyes met mine, he reached down and hit the off switch.

"Oh, Paul. What happened?" I asked.

"The ground just can't hold any more rain," he said, wiping his palms on his jeans. "Water is coming in anywhere it can—even from under the fireplace."

He dragged the Shop-Vac to the back door and tipped it. The contents splashed across the patio and onto the grass.

Our two younger daughters and seven-year-old son, jeans rolled to their thighs, knelt in the water, using plastic cups to scoop as much as they could into buckets. Seeing their willingness to help spurred me to action, and I quickly removed my shoes and rolled up my jeans. I stepped into the water and drew a sharp breath, surprised at how cold it was.

The *scoop-dump-scoop* beat a steady rhythm around me. As we bailed, I sighed. Nothing had seemed to go right for us since my husband had lost his job. For two months, he'd sent résumés to companies all over the city and still was unemployed.

As we waited for doors to open, I felt God showing me something I'd tried to ignore for years. Although I'd accepted Christ as my Savior when I was twenty-one years old, I had seldom, if ever, really trusted him. But this year, God was directing my attention to the children of Israel.

It had started the first week of spring. Over and over again I saw them—in a novel I'd casually picked up at the library . . . in my youngest daughter's schoolwork . . . in an e-mail from a friend. Everywhere I turned, I heard about their walk across the Red Sea, their cries for water and food in the desert, and their crossing of the Jordan River into Jericho. I couldn't look at a glass of water without thinking of them!

The old Bible stories had been read to me often when I was a child. I'd read them myself numerous times. But this was different.

As I dumped cupfuls of water into my bucket, I thought about the night we'd watched the old movie *The Ten Commandments.* I'd seen the epic many times, but this year, it was with new eyes and a heart ready to receive. I'd never before considered the people's grumbling to be a lack of trust. Their lack of gratitude was clear, but I hadn't noticed their unwillingness to trust God. When reading the biblical account of the Exodus, I'd thought the consequences they suffered for their lack of faith had always seemed rather harsh. But as the familiar story had unfolded on the screen that night, I saw anew the choices the Israelites made, and it began to sicken me. They chose repeatedly to trust in things or people or circumstances rather than God.

And in every scene, I could feel myself part of the crowd. I had to admit I'd been like the Israelites nearly all my adult life—grumbling, complaining, accusing, mistrusting. I would pray for guidance but rarely wait for an answer. Instead, I'd go directly to Plan B—my plan, for my life.

After watching the movie that night, I knew I needed to repent, and my heart cried out to Jesus to change me, help me, make me able to trust him. The following Sunday, our pastor challenged us to recognize our Deliverer. That statement pierced my heart. For days I asked myself, *Who is my Deliverer? How many times has God come through for me over the years?* Countless times. But just like the children of Israel,

I was always quick to forget how he'd rescued me. Instead of remembering the victories, I saw only the giants in front of me, the walls of doubt towering above me like the walls of Jericho.

Now, something was changing. Day by day, I felt God stirring my heart, changing my attitude, my way of thinking, my opinions. Who is my Deliverer? Not a paycheck-providing company. The Lord is my Rock and my Fortress and my Deliverer. I was finally getting it.

As I carried my bucket to the back door and dumped the murky water onto the grass, I turned and saw my children bailing together and Paul still hard at work with the Shop-Vac. I was surprised my stomach wasn't clenching with worry. As I reseated myself on the stepstool, I took a quick emotional inventory. Besides worry, another emotion was curiously absent: fear. *Could it be I'm finally learning to trust you? In everything? Oh, I want that, Jesus. Trusting in myself isn't working. I want to trust in you and only in you.*

The lights flickered. Everyone stilled and looked up at the ceiling, waiting. The lights flickered again. "Oh Lord, no," I breathed. "Please, no." And with that breath, the lights went out.

My husband's voice broke through the blackness. "This is kind of funny when you think about it." After a brief second of silence, all of us were laughing and talking at once, feeling our way to the stairs, searching for candles and matches and flashlights. The next time we made it back down to the family room, the water had risen. With no electricity to operate the Shop-Vac, we'd have to rely on bailing alone, slowing the process down considerably. We decided to enlist the help of friends and made quick phone calls.

We all began scooping water again, determined to make as much progress as we could before help arrived. Fifteen-year-old Chelsea had her bucket next to mine. She tucked a strand of hair behind her ear and smiled at me. "This is exciting!"

I sat back on my stool, stunned. How in the world could she possibly think that? We were sitting in near darkness with water up to our ankles! Didn't she understand the long-term effects of this night? the loss of furniture? the cost of replacing the carpet?

Evidently not, because she was still grinning!

Ordinarily, I would've brushed off my daughter's comment as the naïveté of youth, but not this time. When life is difficult, I listen harder. Her words connected with what God had been stirring in my heart for weeks. Chelsea was able to see excitement in what should've been a miserable situation simply because she trusted her parents. She knew her dad was there with his Shop-Vac, and I was there with my bucket. She understood that although she was expected to do her part to help, the final outcome wouldn't be her responsibility. Her mom and dad would take care of the furniture and the walls and the carpet. She would eventually be able to go to bed and rest, but her parents would be up as long as it took. It was all about trust.

Voices in the hallway upstairs signaled that reinforcements had arrived. Soon our family room was full of friends and neighbors, sloshing through the ankle-deep water with us. Eleven-year-old Moriah had turned on her battery-operated radio, and the atmosphere became almost festive. We laughed and joked with one another. My son splashed toward me, his eyes sparkling even in the dimness. "Look, Mommy! I can walk on water!" The room erupted with laughter.

We worked until well past midnight. When the room was suddenly ablaze with light, a shout of triumph went up. I was almost disappointed. Music and candlelight can make even bailing water fun.

With the Shop-Vac running again and the rain easing up, it wasn't long before the flooding was under control. I walked our tired and soggy friends to the door and sent them home with hugs of gratitude.

It was 3 A.M. before my husband and I stumbled into bed. As exhausted as I was, I couldn't stop thinking about all that had happened that night. It felt as if we'd thrown a party rather than survived a flooded basement! My husband didn't have a job, and by morning, my house would smell like a hundred soured bath towels. And yet, my heart was at rest. I knew that in everything I'd been through, Jesus was drawing me to him. I could sense his gentle presence. *Trust me. Trust me.*

I turned over and pulled the comforter up to my chin. For so long, I had tried to live life on my own. But no more. It had taken years for me to finally see my sin of self-sufficiency. It was time I started to trust. I didn't want to be like Peter, looking down at the waves under his feet as he started to sink. I wanted to trust my Deliverer, hang up my bucket, and go to bed.

I smiled into the darkness, remembering when the lights had gone out. What was it that C. S. Lewis had said about darkness? "Why must holy places be dark places?" My smile deepened. "Or wet ones!" I whispered at the ceiling.

I didn't know how we would deal with the effects of the flooding. I didn't know when my husband would find another job. But I did know my Deliverer. The same God who had led the children of Israel through the Red Sea on dry ground would lead me through life, if I would only trust him.

Sleep was just seconds away, but I resisted long enough to breathe a prayer of thanksgiving. Jesus had loved me enough to hold the mirror of truth in front of me. Then, standing beside me, he had given me the courage to look into it.

—Cynthia L. D'Agostino

HOW GOD DEALS WITH A THIEF

"Oh Lord, please either bless these men or get them away from here."

Norma whispered the prayer as she watched three seedy-looking characters wander into the Christian bookstore my husband and I owned. She and Debbie, my daughter, were the only employees at the moment, and both felt very apprehensive.

With a cautious smile, Debbie approached one of the trio, a tall, lanky guy. "May I help you with something?" He ignored her inquiry. His eyes were hidden behind dark sunglasses, but when he looked her way, Debbie felt him sizing her up. He had a scraggly beard and mustache and wore a full-length leather coat. A dusty cowboy hat topped his long hair, which was dyed three colors—red, blond, and sort of purple. He sauntered toward the back of the store.

The other two didn't look as bizarre, but their cocky attitudes made Norma and Debbie just as uncomfortable. They were obviously out to distract the women while their friend scoped out the merchandise.

"So, what kind of music does this place sell? We're in a rock band and always want to keep up with what's new." The comment, from the one who appeared to be the youngest, dripped with sarcasm. He and his cohort laughed.

"You can use the listening center over there," Debbie said, pointing to the area with players and headphones. "We have plenty of demos."

He made no move to check it out, but he and his buddy continued with small talk.

"This here's our bass player," the other one said, nodding toward the young one, "and I play drums. David's the lead guitarist and his woman's our singer—she's got a great voice."

"Where do you perform?" Norma asked, just to say something.

"Oh, here and there. You know, wherever we can make a buck."

Eventually, the tall one headed back, and the other two knew it was their cue to leave. Norma and Debbie watched them climb into a van and drive off. "Do you suppose he took anything?" Debbie asked.

"I doubt he found much that interested him here," Norma replied. "But if he walked out with something, I pray that God uses it somehow to impact his life."

Of course, Debbie and Norma filled my husband and me in on their experience, including a detailed description of the men, particularly the one they referred to as David. We didn't expect to see them again and probably would never know if anything was missing.

A few days later as I worked with a customer, two men came to the door. After a single glance, I recognized David and the one who was surely in his teens from the description Norma and Debbie had given me. I tried to concentrate on the person I was helping while I kept an eye on the newcomers.

I was glad other shoppers were there, and it was reassuring to know that Jerry, my husband, was in the office at the other side of the store. But I really wished he were right beside me at that moment. *Lord, protect me and have your way with these men,* I silently prayed.

They both wandered around, as one by one the customers checked out. I was about to go find Jerry when the two approached the cash register where I stood. My heart began to pound. "May I help you?" My voice trembled with the mundane question.

David looked at his friend and said, "You go on outside. I want to talk to this lady a minute."

I felt like I was in a dream in which no sound could get past the constriction in my throat, though I hadn't actually tried to scream. The one called David took off his sunglasses, and I looked him in the eye.

He lowered his gaze and suddenly seemed very unsure of himself. Almost vulnerable. In a quiet voice he said, "I was here the other day, and I stole some stuff. I want to pay for these and also the things I took then."

I hadn't even noticed that he had stacked several books on the counter.

By then tears had welled up in his eyes. "One of the things I stole was a book. I started to read it, and I could hardly put it down. I've committed my life to Christ because of it."

He tentatively waited for my reaction, but he didn't have to wait long. By then I could barely hold back my own tears. "I'm so happy for you," I told him through a weepy grin. "Everything here belongs to God, to do with as he pleases. It's exciting to know that he used something from our store to help you see you needed a Savior."

He paid for his new purchases, as well as the stolen

merchandise, while we continued to talk. Before he left, I walked around the counter to give him a hug. He was a little startled, but clung to me for a moment, with an obviously unfamiliar emotion that brought a fresh burst of tears. I glanced up in time to see his friend outside the window looking totally confused.

During the following weeks, David came to the store often and became a favorite with all the people who worked there. He seemed so hungry to learn more of God and to spend time with other believers.

He brought his wife, Beth, who told us she, too, had become a Christian. "I couldn't miss the change in him," she said. "You can't believe how different he is! He said it was Jesus, and I knew I needed whatever he had found."

They already realized that the band they were in and the gigs they played in bars would drag them down. The other band members didn't understand, so they teased them about being "Jesus freaks," even during performances.

David and Beth considered other alternatives and asked for advice, but we knew it wasn't our place to try to sway their decision. We just prayed with them and offered encouragement.

"It seems as though the Lord wants us to leave the band," they said, "but neither of us has any other training."

The idea of hearing from God was brand new to them. Their parents weren't really interested, and the only family member who might help was David's grandmother in California. "Grandma's been praying for me all my life," he said. "She'd love for us to come out there, but everything's more expensive there, and we don't have much money."

One day the two of them came in holding hands, with

grins that lit up their faces. "We've quit the band," they told us. Their future held question marks and resources were scant, but to look at them, you'd have thought they owned the world.

"Grandma invited us to stay with her till we can figure out what we're supposed to do," David said. "So we're leaving for California tomorrow."

"We'll always remember you," Beth said as she reached out with a farewell hug. "Our lives are in God's hands now, and we're so excited about what he's doing."

David had changed remarkably since we first met him. His hair was a little shorter and had gone to its natural brown. But the biggest changes were reflected in the peace that radiated from his eyes and the joy on his face. His voice cracked and tears surfaced when we parted. He tried to laugh. "I sure didn't expect this when I came in here that first time!"

Norma had prayed that God would either bless the men or get them out of there. As I hugged David good-bye, I was glad that the same God who reached out to bless a dying thief on a cross is still at work, blessing thieves and drawing them to himself.

—Ardythe Kolb

THE FEDEX KINKO'S MAN . . . AND ME

The hum of machines, the smell of hot paper, the rising tempers, the waiting lines two abreast and growing—lunch hour at FedEx Kinko's copy shop demands patience and a sense of humor. The graying fellow across from me seemed short on both. Slumped inside his long brown coat, he looked like he could use a friend. The thought repeated itself in my head, insisting I do something.

Good heavens, the guy's my age—he'll think I'm coming on to him, I argued.

Still, the prompting lingered. Glumly, he flipped through his originals, rechecked his watch, then exhaled loudly.

"Like waiting for spring in the Midwest," I quipped, nodding toward the register.

His lips quirked, but his eyes, the quiet shade of moss after rain, gazed back without humor.

"I'm copying invitations," I said, waving my masters. "For a party."

OK, that was way too perky. It probably made him feel worse.

"Résumés," he said, raising a dented manila folder. "Lost my job."

"O-o-oh, I'm sorry," I said and meant it. My husband and

I had worked dozens of jobs over our three decades together. I intimately knew the stress—and distress—of transition, with all its hazards and opportunities. Something had always opened up, eventually. Was it because of our faith? Or was it because God is the source of every good thing, for everyone, and loves to provide? The latter, I decided.

Maybe hearing this would encourage the stranger, but I wasn't sure how to introduce the Almighty into small talk at FedEx Kinko's.

The man had faced forward again, so I edged closer. "I can appreciate what you're going through because . . ."

He stared back, eyes widening, and I faltered. What did I know about this guy's life? Maybe he'd embezzled from his company. Or been fired for groping a coworker. I stepped back, increasing the space between us. Overhead, the fluorescent lights hummed, one tube over the counter randomly strobing. It buzzed now and then, like those neon bug machines at the old drive-in theater back home. Meanwhile, neither of our lines had budged. The man lifted his eyebrows as if daring me to finish my sentence. Beneath them, his eyes looked darker and didn't blink.

"Er, we've lost jobs too," I said. "My husband and I." At least he knew I was married now, but my spurt of courage fizzled. Shrugging a little, I clammed up.

"What's a middle-aged guy to do?" he muttered.

Was he talking to himself or asking me? Ahead, customers peeled away from the two lines like cards from a deck. The stranger and I moved in tandem toward the counter. If I was going to say more, I'd have to hurry.

"This'll probably sound crazy," I ventured, "but I'm going

to pray that God leads you to a good job. It's worked for us every time."

He stared a moment longer, shook his head as if to clear it, then shuffled his papers, obviously relieved when the cashier called, "Next?" He handed in his order, and he ignored me when he left, a stack of résumés bulging his beat-up folder.

Not very smooth, but please, God, come through for this guy.

Over the next few weeks, I prayed for the Kinko's man, prayed he'd find work he'd enjoy. Then, one day while I was leaving a grocery store miles from Kinko's, I noticed a figure slouching near the watermelons. I peered through the strings of balloon bouquets near the lilies. It was the FedEx Kinko's man—the same long, brown, belted coat, the same defeated posture. He stood third in line for the free blood-pressure clinic. Not a good sign. Holding my sack higher, I hurried past, not wanting to be recognized.

Go back, that familiar voice in my head urged. *Complete the loop.*

I gazed toward the upholstered safety of my sedan, biting my lip. I would have bitten my nails, too, if I'd had time. What if he was still unemployed? Maybe he'd declared bankruptcy, and the wife I'd imagined for him had filed for divorce. On the other hand, I had to know if I'd been right to follow my first nudge. I'd thought at the time that it was God talking to me. If so, it could be again.

No more lip chewing, then, and no more selfish, white knuckled stalling. With groceries clutched to my chest, I approached him.

"Um, hello. We talked once, at FedEx Kinko's." The balloons bobbled nearby in a draft from the door. He was looking blank, and I hurried on, speaking softly so the others in line around him wouldn't hear.

"I've been praying for you. I just have to know: Did you find a job?"

"Oh, it's you." The man slouched even more, and his eyes crinkled at the corners.

Shoot, he was going to cry, and it was my fault. I shifted the groceries to my hip, caught a potent whiff of lilies, and immediately thought of funerals, grieving, depression. As if in sync with my morbid imagination, he pulled a hankie from his pocket, sneezed into it, then blew his nose.

"Allergic," he explained, nodding toward the flowers. He refolded the monogrammed square. Then he straightened, looking for a moment almost boyish. "My new job's great. Pays twice as much as the old one."

"I . . . oh, wow!" I felt as if I'd swallowed the balloons, as if helium were bubbling through my bloodstream. "That's fantastic! Boy, God really cares about you." Then, as an afterthought, I added, "It is personal, you know."

"Next," the nurse called, unrolling the gray rubber cuff with its Velcro strip.

The man glanced at her, then back at me. "I, um . . . well, guess I should thank you."

"Oh, no," I said. "Not me. God's the One to thank, the One who did it." My excitement made this come out louder than I had intended. Several people turned and stared at me, then at him.

"God," he said, and the word sounded small in his mouth, its edges crimped. "Ah, yeah—OK." He shrugged at the others in line, as if to show I was harmless.

I'd like to report that he knelt down and prayed, right

there beside the balloons and the melons and the hypertensive people in line who were anxiously waiting with rolled-up sleeves. He didn't. But maybe he thinks about God now and then. Maybe he wonders.

Sure, he got the job, but I walked away with something deeper, more lasting: the joy of obeying God despite modest results. I'm a little more daring about speaking out now when it seems heaven is tugging at my sleeve—I've learned that people aren't going to react as negatively as I might imagine when I remind them that God cares about them. Besides, maybe the story's not over yet. I do know our two encounters boosted my faith in prayer and action—which is why I've been praying about his allergies lately. Also his blood pressure.

—Laurie Klein

THE CANYON

Rain threatened as we neared the entrance of the Grand Canyon. I thought I heard Alan breathe something about hoping the Canyon wasn't fogged in, as if saying it louder might make it a reality. I dismissed the thought, trusting that the Lord would not have brought me here only to miss seeing the Canyon in all its grandeur. Pretty soon we joined a long line of cars at the park entrance.

Then the nice lady in the park station booth leaned over and said, "I need to let you know before you pay your twenty dollars that the Canyon is completely fogged in today."

There it was, our dread confirmed.

I had lived and sweat in Phoenix, Arizona, for twenty years and had never bothered to see the Grand Canyon, a four-hour drive from my home. Pictures were impressive and satisfied what little curiosity I had. So why now, after twenty years of living a thousand miles away in the Northwest, had this destination lured me?

Just a month or two earlier, my husband of twenty-three years had walked out of my life, heading to "greener pastures" and the open arms of a woman I'd mistaken for a friend. Though our marriage was not perfect, I'd always believed things would improve with time, prayer, and better communication. I'd thought we'd honor the commitment we'd made to each other in the little pioneer church where we were married.

Overworked and drifting from God, we let time erode our relationship. Through the years, I had literally cried out for a restorative breeze to blow through our home and bring us to a healed and happy place. A wind came—different, not fresh, not good at all. It lingered, until one night a large man knocked on my door and handed me divorce papers. A court-appointed process server delivered my answer to years and years of fervent, gut-level prayer.

In the shock and stillness following, God had to tell me many times to release my grip, that he was allowing this change. But I had held on so tenaciously for so long that my life, my thoughts, and everything I had become were geared only for rescue, and I refused to accept that things couldn't work out. What hadn't I said? How could I reword things to force a mutual understanding? But my attempts at control were only props, a simulator. I could push buttons and pull levers till I made myself crazy, and nothing would change. There was no connection except to God, and he was in control, not I.

The weeks after the breakup were filled with prayer, books, friends, tears, good counsel, and more tears. God wrapped me in his arms and became my covering, my constant companion. I would never trade those bittersweet autumn days.

During that time, visions of the Canyon began making appearances in my life, inviting me to view its grandeur. I needed a change of scenery and sensed that a rendezvous awaited.

First, I saw the newspaper article with my morning coffee—a sprawling photo of the Canyon. The article revealed how people facing a personal crisis often found some healing effects while visiting places of such majestic proportions. The message came through loud and clear, especially when the author shared that he'd gone to the Grand Canyon when his marriage of twenty-three years had ended. Twenty-three. Not fourteen or twenty-one, but twenty-three, exactly the same as mine.

Then, I remembered an invitation from my brother, Alan, who had remained in Phoenix. "Let's visit the South Rim of the Canyon the next time you're down," he'd coaxed.

Spring break would offer a week off from my job at school and be the perfect time to go, so I began eagerly planning our adventure.

And now I sat in the car, not letting the park lady's words dash my hope. We quietly opted to pay the twenty dollars and go in, since we'd come so far.

The weather was cold and rain sprinkled and we were without umbrellas. I was from Oregon, after all, where an umbrella labels one a tourist. We ended up *wet* tourists. As we neared the edge, we peered into a giant bowl of undulating gossamer. We had only an educated guess about the bowl part, because it was so socked in with fog that it could have been the Grand Plain for all we could see.

We joined herds of people inside the lodge and tried to cheer ourselves with cups of hot chocolate. The vendors seemed content. All of us untimely visitors stared blankly at row after row of turquoise jewelry and colorful mugs teasing us with pictures of the Canyon on them. I'd seen pictures. What I really wanted was to stand breathless and enlightened before the real thing.

I overheard a gift store clerk exclaim to another guy how this storm was a thick whopper that stretched all the way to California. He made it very clear that it wasn't likely to blow over anytime soon. I felt cheated as I walked outside, but the same stubborn hope that had kept me clinging to a dying marriage compelled me to look again. Standing at the rim as if before God himself, I prayed and told God I believed he could sweep away the fog and reveal the glory of these deeply worn walls if he desired so that I would receive what he had brought me here for.

We tried to make the most of our visit by taking in the art exhibits and various historical displays, but we kept sneaking back to peek at the Canyon.

Pulling our jackets closer against the spitting rain, I wondered if I was just ignorant of the Canyon's habits during inclement weather—or was God stirring the kettle?

The billowy, thick mass began to roll and move, peaking and tearing apart in small, uneven fragments like cotton candy—just enough to reveal tantalizing glimpses of the far-reaching other side. A slice of striated color would appear briefly and be gone. I could have stood there all day enjoying the gradual unveiling, but I didn't have to. The fresh breeze I had prayed for came and swept through the Canyon, exposing its spectacular beauty as it showed itself a clear testament to the Creator God's love and faithfulness.

Isaiah 44:22 says, "I have swept away your sins like a cloud. I have scattered your offenses like the morning mist. Oh, return to me, for I have paid the price to set you free."

The breeze blew through my life as well, carrying off the fog that kept reminding me of the past's chaos and confusion. My frustration had been deep and all-consuming at times, distorting the truth and full of formidable shapes and specters. My attempts at battling them were no more than shadow boxing. I'd spent morning after morning praying Scripture over the situation, using it like an antibiotic. But God, in his perfect timing, now swept the dross of my past away to reveal the strong beauty and promise of his perfect plan, which had been there all the time, just as he did with the fog in the Canyon.

—Peggy Overstreet

CAUGHT UNDER A CAR!

My one-year-old, Alisha, cried her new word, "Hi," for the hundredth time that afternoon as I drove into our town house parking lot. It was past three o'clock, so I surmised the mail must have arrived. Normally, I would park the car near my town house, walk down to the mailbox a block away, and retrieve any letters I had received. But on a whim, I stopped in front of the stack of mailboxes. The day was nice for October: a cloudless, beautiful, Indian summer day.

I opened our mailbox with my key, took out the letters, and perused them before walking away. Nothing important. Because I was self-employed, the mail was important to me as I waited for business leads and checks. I'd struggled for months at this new work and felt at times that I'd misread what I believed was God's guidance to try the venture. At times I wondered if he even knew what was happening.

Now, a strange, scraping sound diverted my attention.

"Help!" a man screamed.

I turned, my heart jumping into overdrive, trying to spot the problem. A red Honda was rolling straight back on the pavement to my left. The scraping sound intensified, like a rubber mat being pulled across concrete.

"Help me! Help me!"

Two elderly Burmese people I recognized as neighbors hobbled down the path toward me. The old man cried, "He's under the car! My son! He's caught under the car!"

Instantly, I bent and saw Khin U, a man of about forty-six, pinned under the rear axle of the car. The car dragged backward, leaving white lines on the black pavement. Khin couldn't move. He couldn't breathe. Still the car rolled backward. I felt frozen in time, in space.

Strangely, my mind filled with the eerie calm I'd felt once before when an accident had occurred. It was a dream-like sensation, yet I felt intent, in control.

I dropped my letters and ran to try to stop the car. Before I reached it, the car slowed, then halted because of the pressure of Khin's body underneath it. Inside my mind, words registered: *Put on the brake!*

Mentally, a sharpness of perception struck me, almost as though being guided. I knew exactly what to do.

Mrs. U caught me by the arm and cried, "Please help him! Please get him out!" Khin's father gestured and shrieked. I hurried around the car, opened the door, and jumped in. The stick shift sat in neutral, with the brake off. I thought Khin must have forgotten to put it in park before he got out and walked behind the vehicle. Then he was sucked under when it rolled backward.

I rammed the gear shift into park and searched for the brake.

Khin wheezed, "Please!"

Mrs. U screamed, "He can't breathe. Please hurry!"

I thought I might be able to drive the car off him. I shouted out the window, "I'm going to start the engine. I might be able to drive the car off his chest. Very slowly."

I wasn't sure it would work. I'd keep my foot on the brake and just ease it. But I had to move quickly, too. I turned the key. The old man yelled, "Be careful! My son! My son!"

The engine started. I eased the shift into drive, with my left foot ramming the brake hard toward the floor. Then I eased off on the brake and just touched the gas.

"Aiee!" Mrs. U was frantic.

As the car lurched slightly forward, Khin screamed. I knew it wouldn't work. He was pinned. I'd only drag him forward.

I jammed the stick back into park and jumped out. There had to be a way.

Mrs. U shouted again, "Oh God, he's going to die! Please hurry! He can't breathe."

I hurried around the car and motioned to the old man. "Help me try to lift it off him."

I yelled to Khin, "See if you can scoot yourself out as we lift."

Khin shook his head, wheezing, "It's crushing my chest."

The car was too heavy. To get the axle off him, we needed to lift the rear wheel off the ground. I knew it was impossible with only the two of us, and probably even with several more.

I peered around. Mr. Haag, a neighbor, was running toward us. "I called 9-1-1!" he shouted. "They'll be here in minutes." But time was running out.

Khin choked again, "Please . . . please."

I searched the lot for something. My eyes spotted my own car, with Alisha still sitting in her car seat. Just a week before, I'd had a flat tire. After changing it, I had simply tossed the equipment into the trunk. My Toyota jack was particularly easy to use, a leverage lift that worked by a screw pulling the triangled sides together. I'd often changed tires in two or three minutes. It was right there on top, in easy reach.

"You must have planned this one, Lord," I murmured as I sped to my nearby car, opened the trunk, and whipped out the jack. Mr. Haag explained to Khin what I was doing. I placed the jack under the frame of Khin's Honda and began twisting the handle as quickly as I could. Mrs. U stood anxiously next to me. "Will it work?"

In less than five seconds we knew. Khin moved.

"I can breathe," he yelled.

"As I lift, scoot yourself out. Mr. Haag will help you," I directed. I wound the jack higher and higher. Mr. Haag grabbed Khin under the armpits and pulled him out from beneath the axle. In twenty seconds, he stood shakily next to the car, grinning. His skinny body was soaked with sweat. His white dress shirt was shredded. Five huge patches of abraised skin stood out on his shoulders, red and white with flecks of gravel imbedded. I winced. It looked raw and painful. But Khin gave me his hand. "You saved my life."

I laughed as tears burned my eyes. "Praise God, man. I thought you were gone."

I shook his hand, then let the jack down, noticing the sweat under my shirt and my pounding heart. For the first time, I fought back a rush of emotion.

Mr. Haag inspected Khin's back and told him he was the luckiest man alive that day. Khin only smiled. "I'm all right. I can't believe it! I'm all right."

He didn't seem to be in pain. His face shone with gratitude, and his wife gripped his hand, weeping. Moments later, an ambulance and a policeman arrived. Khin was taken to a nearby hospital and bandaged. Someone else drove the car back to its parking space, and I put the jack back in my car.

When I turned around, I noticed three off-white lines, about fifteen feet long, where Khin's shirt and back had rubbed off on the macadam. I looked at the pavement again and winced. But I thought of Mr. Haag's words: "Luckiest man alive."

"No," I said to myself. "God had it all figured out."

I picked up my scattered mail and checked it again, hoping I'd missed something. Still no good news.

As I clambered back into my car, Alisha cried, "Hi!" and I laughed. "You don't even know what happened, do you?"

She said, "Hi," again and waved.

Later that afternoon, I found Khin's broken glasses by the curb and took them to his house. His father came out, thanked me for saving Khin's life, and bowed several times. I said, "I think God was watching over the whole thing."

I tried to explain my idea—how I had just happened to park at the mailbox, how I was able not to panic, how my thoughts remained clear through the whole situation, how the jack was available at just the right moment.

He didn't seem to understand. But as I walked away, I thanked the Lord. A rush of emotion filled me as I returned to my house and picked up Alisha. She gazed into my eyes, said, "Dada, hi!" and giggled.

I laughed and swung her around. I decided I wouldn't worry about the self-employment. Undoubtedly the Lord God had that under control too. I knew in time I'd see his providence just as I'd seen it that day with a neighbor caught under his car.

—Mark R. Littleton

DID HE JUST SAY WHAT I THINK HE SAID?

The moment comes in every parent's life when he or she is sorry that a child ever learned to talk.

Perhaps it is the moment when the child announces, in the solemn silence of a Sunday morning service, "Daddy, I gotta go potty!"

Or perhaps it's the moment when the dear little boy explains to your seventy-two-year-old grandmother exactly where mommy's new baby is waiting to be born, how the new baby will get outside its hiding place, and what the proper name is for each anatomical part involved in the process. Most likely, however, it is the moment when the child utters his first expletive.

You'll be sitting together in the living room, enjoying a quiet evening in front of the TV with your husband while your child plays happily with his toys. Suddenly, a tiny voice shatters the cozy ambience with the utterance of a single shocking syllable.

The word sort of hangs there like one of those conversation balloons in a comic strip. You look at your husband. Your husband looks at you. You both look at your offspring, the child who has been—until now—your hope for the future, your pride and joy, your testament to the triumph of humankind.

Then you and your husband turn toward each other again, and one of you says in disbelief, "Did he just say what I think he said?"

The foul-mouthed little fiend, meanwhile, has returned to his toys and is blissfully unaware of the bomb he just dropped on his now shell-shocked parents.

No matter how careful we are, our children will inevitably be exposed to an array of four-letter words. On TV, even the gentlest sitcoms allow an occasional *#!@ to slip through. In the grocery store or on the street, helpful citizens offer colorful—and loud—vocabulary lessons every day. And in the neighborhood, friendly youngsters are eager to demonstrate their command of gutter talk.

It seems to be a rule that once these words are planted in the psyche of an innocent child, they take root, blossom, and reproduce. And they remain firmly embedded in the deepest recesses of a child's brain, waiting to spring forth again and surprise the socks off unsuspecting mommies and daddies.

The funny thing is that, most of the time, the child has no idea what these words mean, particularly if he is very young. He hears a new word, notices the interesting effect it has on peers and parents, and tucks it away for future reference.

A parent is fortunate indeed if the child exercises his new vocabulary for the first time at home, in private. A discerning parent can then deal with the issue in a calm, controlled manner: "Darling, that is an interesting word you used to describe your frustration with the broken fire truck. I'm sure you derived a great deal of satisfaction from expressing your anger so colorfully. However, that is a word our family does not feel is appropriate, even if Uncle Bob did say it when he hit his thumb with the electric staple gun last week. It is a very naughty word, a word which you must never, ever use again. Mommy is very proud of you, though, for learning a new word and knowing the proper context for its use. Would you like some ice cream?"

This is, of course, in contrast to the old-fashioned response: a shriek of horror from Mom, anger from Dad, and a mouthful of soap for the kid.

Unfortunately, it is quite common for children to try out their new words in public. All within earshot turn toward you and your child, and you can tell from the looks on their faces that they assume he learned those words from you. You want to protest, "Honest! I have no idea where he picked this up! I've never used that word! I don't even know what it means!"

You feel the color rising slowly from your neck, over your cheeks, and up your forehead. You know that you are now three shades of scarlet. You look at your child as though he has sprouted horns and a tail, which you think might be the next stage in his metamorphosis—sort of like the naughty boy in *Pinocchio* who turned into a donkey.

Your child, meanwhile, is relishing your reaction. He isn't quite sure what caused such a stir, but he wants to figure it out so that he can use the word again when he wants some excitement.

You stare at him for the longest time, trying to decide whether to cry or scream. And then you start to feel strangely sad. You realize that you cannot protect your child from all the evil out there in the world. He's going to hear bad words. He's going to see bad things. He's going to experience pain and sorrow. He will be hurt, emotionally and physically.

No matter how hard you try, you can't shield him, because these things are all part of life. You can only give your child to God and ask God to protect and step in where you can't.

So you hug your child close, and you explain that some words are simply unacceptable. They are words meant to hurt people, words that tell people you have more anger than love in your heart. They are words that make God sad. You instruct your child that he must never use those words. If he does, he will have to pay the consequences—a time-out in his room, missing his favorite show, or whatever you deem appropriate for such a misdemeanor. After you send him off to play, you go somewhere and cry because he has lost some of his innocence.

And there's not a thing you can do about it. Except turn to God.

—Rhonda Wheeler Stock

LOST AND FOUND

The walls of the empty room echoed as I swallowed the lump in my throat. I couldn't delay any longer. I had to leave the last key to our dream home inside and lock the door behind me.

Five years before, my husband, LeRoy, and I had searched for months for the perfect home. Three steps inside this house, I'd stood, riveted. "I think we're home," I had whispered.

Gazing out the wall of windows that ran from the floor to the eighteen-foot cathedral ceiling, LeRoy had smiled and nodded. After several minutes he had asked, "Do you suppose we ought to look at the rest of the house before we make an offer to buy it?"

Through the years, the house had met our needs perfectly. But the setting is what had captured our hearts. Just beyond the windows, gorgeous wood ducks floated on the river. Wind whispered through the aspens. We never lost our wonder at watching otter and deer, woodpeckers and wild turkeys, chickadees and hummingbirds, eagles and great blue herons. Each spring Canada geese reclaimed the lawn as a nursery for their fluffy yellow goslings.

We'd planned to enjoy this retreat for the rest of our lives. But our income had plummeted along with a sagging economy. We'd felt forced to put up a for-sale sign and to accept an unreasonably low offer.

I finally coerced myself to lay that last house key in the drawer under the kitchen phone jack. Outside, I pulled the door almost closed, then stood there, paralyzed.

Those walls had housed our happiest years. The setting had inspired us. Our dreams had come to life there.

"You've got to do it!" I finally blurted. I pulled the locked door, and the latch clicked into place. Despair then hit like a tidal wave.

When my tears eased enough for me to see the road, I headed our van eastward. LeRoy had gone ahead to a temporary job near the home of our dear friends, Lawrence and Jean, who lived close to the Canadian border. He and I planned to meet at Lawrence and Jean's and spend several days with them.

The miles whirred by . . . and by . . . and by. I tried to think of the future. But living who-knows-where in a travel trailer for who-knows-how-long didn't appeal to me. All I could see in the rearview mirror was the haven we'd just lost. I wavered between feeling distraught and numb. Had I left my peace, too, behind that locked door?

"At least I can talk to Jean," I consoled myself. "She'll understand. She's refreshed herself in the beauty and peace of our retreat."

A millisecond later those words punched me like a heavyweight boxer's glove. "No!" I gasped. "It's not ours!" The tears gushed again.

After six hours of driving, I arrived at what I thought was our friends' home. But when I crawled stiffly out of the van and started up the sidewalk, the happy faces of two children appeared behind the screen door. Jean and Lawrence had no children in their home. Getting closer, I saw an unfamiliar Hispanic man and woman in the living room. Was I at the right house?

Just then Jean bounded to the door. "You made it! Come on in!"

Right away, Jean introduced me to Pedro and Juanita and their six- and four-year-olds, Maria and Juan. Throughout the evening, Lawrence and Jean strained to understand and speak a few words of Spanish. Their guests struggled with English. Eventually, "Good night" and *"Buenas noches"* flew back and forth, and the guests descended the basement stairs toward a spare bedroom.

"Who are they?" I asked Jean. "What's going on?"

"They're refugees from Guatemala," she answered. She saw my puzzled expression and continued. "We met them at church. They were camping in the church basement with other Central American refugees waiting to immigrate into Canada. We offered to let them stay with us. They wouldn't at first—didn't want to impose. A couple of weeks later, they agreed."

Jean sensed the questions in my mind. "Pedro and his father were business partners," she went on. "Several years ago, their competitor threatened the life of Pedro's father. A few days later, he disappeared—assumed assassinated.

"Pedro's business continued to flourish, while that of his competitor floundered. Finally, this same man threatened to kill Pedro.

"Pedro immediately searched for a car," Jean continued. "He bought a bullet-riddled '56 Chevy that didn't run. He purchased a Ford engine—the only one he could find that he thought he could make work. He transformed the Ford drive-train into a makeshift steering column. Pedro worked night and day on the car while Juanita quietly sold their household goods for whatever she could get.

"Many mechanical adaptations and four days after the threat on his life, Pedro and Juanita took Maria and Juan for a ride in their 'new' car. That 'test drive' took them three thousand miles, to our home. They check at the Canadian border nearly every day to see if their entrance has been approved.

"All they own is in one small suitcase, plus a small bag of toys some relatives in Los Angeles gave the kids."

When I went to bed, sleep eluded me. Light drapes at the open window fluttered in a cool breeze. The events of the day and evening filled my mind, and slowly, the significance of losing our dream home paled. Sure, we'd lost a few thousand dollars, and we didn't have a clue what the future held. But we had each other. We'd not been cut off from family or friends. And we had a storage unit full of belongings. I thanked God for our blessings and asked him to comfort and bless Pedro and Juanita.

In the morning, sorrow for Pedro and Juanita tore at my heart. But Pedro and Juanita didn't need sympathy. They lived each day cheerfully and selflessly. Sometimes, Juanita cooked delicious Guatemalan specialties. After meals, Pedro often won the race to do dishes. And he already recognized the squeak of the closet door where the vacuum cleaner was kept. Whenever he heard it, he'd hurry down the hall. "I do. I do," he'd say.

With everyone helping, the cooking, cleaning, and other household chores were finished quickly. That gave us more time to visit. We English speakers learned Spanish words.

The Spanish speakers increased their English vocabulary. We drew pictures and motioned with our hands and sometimes laughed together till our sides ached.

During the five days we three families shared, neither Pedro nor Juanita whined or cried over what they'd lost. They didn't measure life by that loss. They enjoyed and thanked God for the treasures they still possessed—life, faith, hope.

As my husband and I drove away, Pedro, Juanita, Maria, and Juan smiled and waved from the porch along with Lawrence and Jean.

"God," I prayed aloud as we turned the corner, "whenever I start to feel sorry for myself, would you please remind me of Pedro and Juanita?"

Over and over again through the two years my husband and I lived in a travel trailer, remembering Pedro and Juanita's example helped me make an often-difficult choice—to enjoy the days and thank God for our blessings instead of bemoaning yesterday's losses. When I chose to look for God's hand in my life, I discovered blessings large and small that I had overlooked. I began again to see God's leading . . . and to trust him when I couldn't see.

I'd lost my peace when we lost our home. I found it in thankfulness and trust.

—Helen Heavirland

SLIPPED STITCHES

"Oh, no! Is there any way to fix these little holes in my scarf?" asked twelve-year-old Brynna. "I must have dropped some stitches. It's the first scarf I've knit, and I wanted to give it to my mom for Christmas."

As her former schoolteacher, I'd taught Brynna how to knit for a fun after-school hobby. Awkward young fingers were being trained to wield yarn and "sticks" into something wearable. With her face bowed over the yarn as if in prayer, I watched as each stitch slowly evolved. I encouraged each tense movement of her hands with a word of praise.

Now, three months later and a finished scarf in her hand, I assured her, "Honey, your mother will love your scarf just the way it is. It's your first effort, and it's just right. She will be so proud of you. She'll wear your scarf to warm her neck and her heart because it was a gift from you."

I didn't realize that in just three weeks I would face my own "dropped stitches."

I had been invited to lead worship at a large conference in Germany. *Wow!* I thought. *Am I up to this?*

I wrestled with accepting the offer because I felt so inadequate to the size of the task. I had led worship in my church, but never abroad. I needed time to pray. I needed to talk to those who knew me and understood my skills.

"Go!" said my husband. "I'll take care of the dogs."

"What an opportunity!" said my best friend. "I believe you can do it."

"Absolutely!" my pastor said with a grin. "Can't wait for the good report when you get home."

I accepted the invitation because of an increasing peace in my heart and because of the confidence of those who loved me. Soon joy and anticipation replaced fear and anxiety.

I practiced and prayed. I organized and prayed. I recruited musicians and prayed.

This will be perfect, I thought. First, I found the perfect pianist. Then, I found the perfect music. That took months of painful deliberation. I even found the perfect travel wardrobe. Now, surely, the rest would fall into place.

The pianist and I flew from the United States to Germany and joined eight other musicians who would be participating in the conference. They were eager to serve the Lord with their musical talents. We all received our rooms and our schedules.

Oh my, I thought, *we have only one afternoon to rehearse together before the big first night of the weeklong event.*

The next day, we musicians scrambled to find our music and our places onstage. We packed the rehearsal full, hoping we had the information we needed. I remembered to keep my heart centered in my love for Jesus, and I prayed for his anointing. Then I instructed my team, "Remember, above all things, that we are here as worshipers, not just musicians."

Soon, five hundred women and thirty-six pastors filled the auditorium for the annual conference of Protestant

Women of the Chapel from all the military bases in Europe. More than thirty denominations were represented. Many hearts had come to be refreshed and to seek the Lord. Many of the women were wives of soldiers. The rest *were* soldiers.

In the minutes before we began, I knew we needed God to enable our worship team to flow in unity with so little practice time. Yet, I also felt responsible to keep the loose ends together. I gripped the microphone and sensed the lightheadedness that nervousness can bring. Added to that was jet lag. Would I remember everything a worship leader needs to remember?

I bowed my head and prayed, "Lord, may this worship time be a blessing to you." Then I stepped out in faith.

We began to play our instruments and sing. Amid the praises, I noticed that things were going wrong. The sound system echoed, even though it had been checked out earlier. I announced, "Can anyone in the house fix that?" To my dismay, no one could. The soundman had left. We tried to ignore it, but I was rattled.

Then, I forgot the first word in my solo—a singer's worst fear besides singing off-key. Suddenly, my memory returned, but I slurred the next two words together to make up for the lost beat in the song. I hoped no one would notice.

At various times, the team missed my cues on when to start or stop, and I realized they couldn't see me. I mentally noted to fix that at tomorrow's rehearsal, but for that night, my last hope for a perfect performance dropped like a ball of unwinding yarn.

I looked at the precious faces of God's daughters. They were worshiping the Lord. Their eyes were closed or uplifted. Some shed tears. Some raised their hands, and others knelt.

Gratefully, I continued to sing and to remember that we were the brides of Christ. Our Savior deserved our praise.

We closed in prayer, and I sat. The twenty minutes of worship seemed like a blur to me. I wasn't sure how I had done as a worship leader, but my mistakes were beginning to replay in my mind.

By the end of the evening's program, the list of things that went wrong pinched my joy at being there and made me wonder if I'd misunderstood God by accepting the invitation to come.

Horrible thoughts taunted me: *You don't know what you're doing, and they're going to know it. What made you think that you could do this? You made huge mistakes!*

Then I heard my heavenly Father speak to my spirit: *Thank me for the things that went right. Make a list.*

OK, Lord, I said. As I entered my room, I began to write my list:

I didn't throw up.
I didn't faint.
I didn't fall off the stage or run away.
I didn't forget you or who I am in you.
I did remember to worship you.
I didn't fail to love you and your ladies, and now I'm not going to fail to love myself or give myself grace.

As I continued writing, I began to laugh. Then I remembered Brynna's scarf. I said, "Lord, I dropped some stitches tonight in the gift I wanted to offer you. I wanted it to be a perfect garment of praise. I wanted your women to enter into the Holy of Holies."

Again the Lord spoke to me: *I don't see mistakes. I see heart, just like the parent you described to Brynna who would love her first knitted gift. She wouldn't trade that scarf with the slipped stitches for a cashmere shawl. I wouldn't trade your heartfelt worship for a polished professional performance. Don't look at being perfect, beloved. Just look at me and see that I love you with a perfect love. I am wearing my daughters' gift of worship right now about my neck as a golden scarf.*

I didn't tell Brynna how to pick up slipped stitches. I am sure I will some day. But with my worship leading, I'm not going to worry about dropped stitches again. The Lord didn't attempt to pick them up. He just covered them in his perfect love, freeing me to be myself, his daughter saved by grace.

At the end of the conference I was blessed with these words: "Thank you to our song leader, who led us into the Holy of Holies each night of the conference."

I lifted my eyes to the Lord in thanksgiving and whispered, "Heavenly Father, you are so good. I applaud you for your perfect love in Christ Jesus. It's true that you don't see as man sees—man looks at the outward appearance, but you, Lord, look at the heart" (see 1 Samuel 16:7).

—Gena Bradford

WHERE YOU SLEEP

I've never forgotten how hard the ground was. I was lying face up with a little rock digging into my right shoulder blade. I squirmed, trying to push it aside, but I couldn't budge it through the fabric and plastic beneath me. The bit of gravel wasn't going to move, so I groaned, turned over, and tried to avoid the earthly irritant that lay under our tent.

Could it still be there today, thirty-one years later? I wish I'd kept it. It would be a nice trophy, a reward for sleeping that night on the dry, hard ground.

We were newlyweds, married for just five days. Martha Lynne and I had suffered through a challenging romance of almost four years. We met soon after we started college. But because of financial problems, we ended up in different cities and schools. We nurtured our relationship in old-fashioned ways: snail mail, long-distance phone calls, and visits on weekends and holidays.

When separated, we missed each other painfully. When together, we both celebrated and grieved—it was great to be together again, but we knew it would be over too soon and we'd be apart again.

Now we were married and were traveling cross-country toward our first home! We'd graduated from our respective schools, gathered our nerve, and said, "I do." Rings were on our fingers, and a song was in our hearts. Has anyone ever had such a shining future as we did? We'd spoken an Old Testament pledge to each other at our wedding: "Wherever you go, I will go; wherever you live, I will live. Your people will be my people, and your God will be my God. Wherever you die, I will die, and there I will be buried. May the LORD punish me severely if I allow anything but death to separate us!" (Ruth 1:16-17).

Our first home would be far from Oklahoma, where we'd lived. I was to enter graduate school in Kentucky, a third of a continent away. We packed our few possessions into our car and pulled a small trailer, too. We didn't have much money, so we bought a tent and two sleeping bags to save money on the trip. We'd scouted potential campsites and were sure we'd find campgrounds with soft grassy lawns, clean showers, and maybe even a swimming pool.

We flew along the highway on an August day. We were excited, filled with energy. We drove through the day and into the evening. As the summer sun began to disappear, we watched for the place where we intended to pitch our tent. However, we'd miscalculated our distance, and the campground we sought was farther away than we thought.

It was late—after ten o'clock—when we saw the sign. Though trailers and motor homes were scattered around the lot, no lights were on in the office. A small sign said, "Come on in, get set up, and pay for your stay tomorrow." We were tired so that's what we did.

I'd practiced putting the tent together, but only in daylight. The fabric, stakes, cords, and poles took on weird dimensions in the dark. The grassy lawn we'd imagined was missing. Instead, our only options were patches of dirt and stiff, scrubby weeds. But we'd planned for contingencies.

After getting the tent set up, I began working on two air mattresses. These were the kind a kid would float on in a pool, but our sleeping bags had a special pocket to hold them when they were inflated. We puffed and blew until our mattresses were filled. Exhausted, we collapsed onto our sleeping bags. Last of all, we set an alarm clock to wake us. We needed to get an early start and didn't want to sleep too late.

Sleep came easily. The hectic schedule of the days following our wedding had caught up with us, and we needed rest. We fell asleep quickly and slept deeply.

It was a short night. The next thing I knew, Martha Lynne—my beloved bride of five days—poked me, saying, "It's time to get up. We overslept. The alarm didn't go off."

"Ohh," I groaned. "What time is it?" I didn't want to open my eyes, as that would bring fuller wakefulness. I wanted to sleep some more, regardless of the time.

"It's six-thirty," she said. "Come on, let's get up. I want to go take a shower, pack, and get on the road."

"OK," I said.

I felt much too tired to get up and considered how to get some more shut-eye without starting our first fight.

"Come on," she said. "Let's go."

I didn't answer. She wheedled and begged, all drawing no response from me. Then, she shifted in her bag, and I heard a hissing sound. I realized my air mattress was rapidly losing air.

"What happened?" I asked. "What did you do?"

"Now you have to get up," she said. "Come on."

She had pulled the plug on my mattress, a bit of playful,

loving fun from my cute wife. The mattress emptied much easier than it had filled. In moments I felt the scabby, rough ground through the thin pad of material underneath me.

"You know," I said, "I was going to leave the air in the mattresses and put them in the trailer. That way I wouldn't have to blow them up if we need to sleep in the bags again tonight."

"I'm sorry," she said sweetly. "But if we get up and go, maybe we'll get to where we're going earlier, and we won't have to sleep on the air mattresses again."

I delayed, trying to catch one more little nap. The hard ground was making that a challenge.

Then I heard a gasp. Martha Lynne suddenly sat up, fumbling with the alarm clock as she tried to see its hands.

"Oh, no," she cried. "What did I do?"

She slid from her bag, unzipped the door to the tent, and leaned outside in a search for light.

I was now wide awake.

"What is it?" I asked. "What's wrong?"

"Oh, honey," she said. "I made a mistake." There was a long pause. "It wasn't six-thirty when I looked at the clock. I misread it. It was midnight!"

"Midnight. You mean we had been sleeping for only an hour?"

" I'm sorry. Yes, you're right. We'd been in bed for about an hour. But I woke up and thought we'd slept all night. When I looked at the clock, well . . ."

It was at that moment that I felt the little rock that intersected with the hard, bony plate of my shoulder blade. That stone had probably lain in this place for untold centuries, waiting for me to show up and lie down on it. That chunk of mineral would prick me, poke me, and prevent me from getting a good night's sleep.

"And you let the air out of my mattress," I said.

"Well," she said, thinking. "Let's trade sides. You can have my sleeping bag and air mattress. I'll sleep on the ground."

It was an honest offer, generously made. And had it come from anyone else, I probably would have taken it. But I realized that I couldn't ask my beloved bride to have to deal with that rock.

"No," I said, squirming to find a position to relieve my discomfort. "I want you to have the soft bed. I'm so tired I don't think it will matter what I sleep on."

The earth was my bed that night, and I had my first lesson in forgiving my spouse.

Our sleep habits have never been quite in sync, and I suppose it might have started that night. Moments after her discovery, her slow, steady breathing told me that she was fast asleep. And so—without intending to—we added to our marriage vows that night: "Wherever you sleep, I will sleep, whether on air or a rocky mattress!"

—**Brad Dixon**

MIRACLE IN THE MANGROVES

Skimming along the water's surface in a two-person kayak, I tried to focus on the beautiful scenery and to silence the debate in my mind: *Tell him. . . . Don't tell him; you just started to hurt a few minutes ago. . . . You have no choice, tell him.*

Seated behind me, Richard, my fiancé of one week, paddled the canoe. This strong man loved adventure and travel and was excited to show me the waters of Boca Chica, Florida, where he and his late wife had lived aboard their sailboat.

This was my chance to learn about Richard's history, yet sitting in a kayak turned out to be extremely painful for me. I had permanent nerve and muscle damage to my neck, shoulders, and back from an auto accident three years earlier. Sometimes even sitting in an easy chair was uncomfortable. Sitting in a kayak with no back support was quickly approaching agony. I had to tell Rich this little adventure just wouldn't work. I didn't want to disappoint him, but my aching body left me no choice.

The bright sun shimmered on the water and warmed my face. As I listened to Richard's voice and the quiet splash of his paddle pulling us through the water, I pondered whether I really should marry this wonderful man. I had no doubt that he was the one I had waited for these many years—at forty-two, I'd never been married—but how would we handle the limitations of my chronic pain? Did he really want a woman who couldn't pull ropes on the sailboat or ski with him? Would I be able to keep up with grocery shopping and housework? Since my accident, some of the most basic routines of life challenged me. Until recently, these problems affected only me. Now my limitations would also affect Richard.

Lord, you know me and know my needs. I need your help. Help me ask Richard to turn back the kayak. Help me deal with the pain.

Reminding myself I could be secure in Richard's love, I spoke up. "Umm, hon, I'm really hurting. I can't do this. Sitting without any support is too much for my back."

I bit my bottom lip, unsure about how he would react.

"Oh," he said, and then he was silent.

Fear of losing his love loomed in my mind. Maybe there wasn't enough room in our relationship for my chronic pain. I tried to prepare myself for him to break off the engagement right there as we bobbed on the water's surface like a two-headed duck. Would he ask me to get out of the kayak and out of his life? I held my breath.

"Do you think you could hold out for just five more minutes?" he gently asked.

Quite honestly, I didn't want to, but I trusted that the Lord had heard my prayer. Rich loved me, and I had endured worse pain than this. Attempting to distract myself from my body's protests, I took deep breaths of salt air and watched a bird fly.

"Have you ever seen mangrove trees?" Richard asked.

"No . . ."

"They grow in the water. They're so unique—I want to show them to you, and then we'll head back. OK?"

Trying to hide my discomfort, I agreed, but I was more interested in relief than in mangrove trees. Richard kept paddling as I told myself, *Five more minutes; you can do this for just five more minutes.*

Finally we were gliding beside the mangroves, and I became intrigued by the outlines of the branches. Slender tree limbs emerged from the water's surface, weaving and overlapping in endless patterns, like a puzzle against the blue sky. What unique beauty! Both of us enjoyed the mesmerizing artistry of nature as we drifted along.

Suddenly the beautiful puzzle was broken by some ugly obstruction. As I looked closer, I saw a big, black form.

"Richard!" I could hardly believe my eyes. Could it really be?

True to his personality, Rich calmly replied, "Yes?"

"Did you see that? Did you see it? Go back! Go back!" I could barely talk fast enough.

"Umm, OK . . . why?"

"It was a seat back, a stadium seat! For me! For my back! Go back!"

We paddled back to where my excitement had begun. There, stuck in the branches of some mangrove trees, far from land and completely surrounded by water, was a perfectly good stadium seat—two large, square cushions attached by two straps of webbing created a portable chair to give comfort and back support at a football game, at a picnic, or . . . in a kayak!

Using the kayak paddle to extend his reach, Richard carefully maneuvered the cushions out of the twisted mangrove branches. With a few splashes of water, he cleaned off some dried mud and handed me my new treasure. The webbing was a bit faded and the snaps on the straps were slightly rusted, but otherwise, the seat cushions were in excellent condition—not even a tear from being snagged on the branches.

I opened the seat, slid it under my bottom, and sat back. As I leaned against this miraculous provision of support, the tension in my back and shoulders eased immediately.

"Let's go!" I cried. I was ready for more exploring, and off we went. We finished our delightful kayak tour an hour later.

On the waters of Boca Chica I learned God provides for our needs at just the right moment. When the Israelites needed food in the wilderness, God sent manna. When Abraham was going to sacrifice his son Isaac, God provided a ram in the thicket. And when I was becoming overwhelmed with pain in the middle of a Florida cove, God provided a stadium seat in the branches of a mangrove tree. At that moment I was overwhelmed with the assurance that God would take care of me. I realized he might not always take the pain away, but he would provide a way to get through it.

Richard and I married in the spring of 2004. We take that stadium seat with us to all sorts of places in case I need it. The seat is a reminder to me of God's loving care, even when the pain is discouraging. Many times he provides comfort and encouragement through my dear husband. I have a reminder that God will always provide what I need to get through this life of chronic pain—he blessed me with my wonderful husband, Richard *Payne.* Not only is the Lord faithful, he has a sense of humor.

—Leslie J. Payne

ROOM FOR ONE MORE

Sounds of a newborn baby escaped through the closed door—our grandson's first cry. My husband and I embraced in the hospital corridor. We'd waited seven years for a grandchild. I had hoped for a girl, but I followed the nurse in awe when she invited me to come with her to clean up our grandson. What a little miracle, not even six pounds! I fell in love with Jeremiah.

Eighteen months later, my daughter broke the news. "Jeremiah's going to be a big brother."

My spirit soared. As the oldest of seven, I cherished my sibling relationships. But a cloud of apprehension snagged my excitement: Could I love another grandchild as much as I loved Jeremiah? I had battled favoritism from a grandmother of my children and didn't wish that tangle of emotions on anyone.

It will all work out, I told myself. I had harbored the same reservations when expecting my second child, and it had worked itself out the minute I laid eyes on him.

"Mom," my daughter said months later, "would you like to come with me for the ultrasound?"

This was another first. I had to promise that if the doctor revealed the baby's sex, I wouldn't tell a soul.

I crammed beside the gurney in a tiny room that was already crowded with medical equipment. Heather and I talked about how nice it would be if the baby was a girl, but both of us admitted we'd be totally happy with another little boy.

The doctor squeezed along the opposite side of the bed, spread gel across my daughter's swollen abdomen, and ran the sensor from side to side. I stared at blurs of movement on the screen. I was amazed that things had changed so much since I had my kids.

"A little girl," the doctor said. "She's sucking her thumb."

Maybe I needed to go back to the eye doctor. Heather smiled and gave me the "A-w-w-w, look, Mom" look while I strained to detect a single recognizable feature. I could make out the baby's face and hand, but other than that, the details escaped me.

A girl! It sunk in. One of each—a boy and now a girl. Perfect, except for my lingering fear. Could I love this baby as much as I loved Jeremiah? I thought back to my second pregnancy. I put a lid on the concern, knowing that the fear would go away when I met this little thumb-sucking granddaughter.

Months later, Heather called me at work. It was time to put our hospital drill into action. Her husband worked an hour from home and two hours from the hospital. My husband, Rick, and I would drive Heather to the hospital. Our son-in-law, Kraig, would meet us there, and we'd return home with Jeremiah.

Do plans ever go smoothly? The doctor wanted to see her at his office, not the hospital.

"It will be a while," the doctor said. "You might as well go back home."

We joked about it being a practice run, even went

out for lunch before I headed back to work, but I could tell Heather was uncomfortable. Our eyes met, and a flash of unspoken understanding traveled the mother-daughter link. She thought the doctor was wrong. We decided I'd go back to work for the last two hours of the day, and we'd probably spend the evening at the hospital.

I wasn't at my desk more than fifteen minutes when Heather called. Kraig had arrived home.

"We're heading to the hospital. We'll meet you there," she said. "Jeremiah will be with us."

That hour drive to the hospital took forty-five minutes. When Rick and I pulled into the hospital parking lot, I spotted the doctor walking out the front door.

"That was Heather's doctor!" I twisted to watch him get into a car. "Where's he going?"

"Are you sure it was him?" Rick asked.

I had no doubt. We rushed into the hospital. The woman at the reception desk told us the baby had arrived. We sprinted to the room. I'd finally get to meet my granddaughter and push this lingering fear aside.

Heather lay in the hospital bed, hair matted to her head. Two-year-old Jeremiah perched in his father's arms at the side of the bed.

"We almost didn't make it," Heather said. "She was born ten minutes after I walked in the door." Her smile wavered. "She wasn't breathing. The cord was wrapped around her neck and arm."

"She wasn't breathing?" That sick "this happens to other people" feeling grabbed me.

Heather nodded. Tears filled her eyes. "It's a good thing she was born so fast."

"So, she's OK?" Rick wrapped his arm around me.

"They're taking her to All Children's Hospital," my son-in-law said. "They've done X-rays and confirmed meconium aspiration syndrome."

Jeremiah climbed out of his father's arms and toddled across the sterile linoleum. He chattered about his baby sister as he climbed into my arms. I held him tight.

"What does that mean?"

"She had a bowel movement during the birthing process and breathed in tainted amniotic fluid. There's a risk of bacterial infection."

"So where was Jeremiah through all this?" I asked.

Kraig laughed. "I put him on my shoulders." We chuckled a bit, but the underlying tension showed on every face.

A commotion at the door announced the arrival of my new grandbaby, Taylor Anne. Two technicians dressed in blue jumpsuits had wheeled her into the room to say good-bye before heading to All Children's. My helpless granddaughter had a full head of dark hair and a deep pink complexion. Wires and tubes converged in a tangle and made the incubator look like something from a science fiction novel. I peered through the glass separating us, and she opened her eyes. I swallowed hard.

How could this happen, God? Emotional walls shot into place to barricade my heart from hurt. If I didn't let myself get close, I could handle it if she didn't make it.

They rolled the rectangular glass box next to the bed. Heather rested her hand against the glass. "Good night, Taylor. Daddy's going with you." My throat constricted with emotion while I hugged Jeremiah.

Kraig kissed Heather and followed the incubator to the ambulance.

The room felt empty. We stood around the bed and chatted. My daughter's eyes connected with mine. We traded unspoken concerns. "It will be OK," I said, praying silently that I was right.

Jeremiah fussed. He'd had quite a day. I checked my watch. Almost nine o'clock. "I guess I should get him home." I shifted his weight to my left arm and leaned to hug Heather. "I don't really want to leave you here like this."

"I'll be all right."

She understood, but that didn't make it any easier to walk out the door.

Her dad leaned and kissed her on the forehead. "We'll see you tomorrow morning, bright and early."

I put on my best front, said one last good-bye, and stepped into the hall, where I fell into silent sobs.

The next morning, the doctor released Heather early. My husband, Jeremiah, and I picked her up, and we were on our way to All Children's by 8:30. Heather looked exhausted. I sat, helpless, wondering what the day would bring and asking God for strength and wisdom.

Heather and Kraig stayed at the hospital. I took the week off work, and Rick and I took turns going up to see our granddaughter and allowing Jeremiah to visit his parents.

I followed the narrow corridor, walking past windows displaying babies tiny enough to fit in my palm, and realized how fortunate we all were when I slipped into Taylor's room. At 7 lbs., 4 oz., she looked like a healthy, normal baby, sleeping with her head on Heather's shoulder—except for the wires connecting her to machines.

Heather explained all the technical medical details as she rocked gently in the chair. "Would you like to hold her?"

I stared at all the monitors and wires connected to Taylor's tiny body. "Is it OK?"

"Sure." She handed the baby to me, showing me how to keep the tubes in the right position. I wanted to care. I did care, but I felt like I was holding a little stranger—an adorable little stranger. *God, please let her be all right.*

Taylor's homecoming was a quiet affair. The family looked forward to getting back to the routine of normal life. Jeremiah loved his sister, and I enjoyed holding her without the wires. Little by little, the baby girl that hurried into this world won my heart. Today, she bounces into the room, and it's hard to believe she had such a rocky start. I cherish her affectionate, outgoing personality and love the way she hunts me down for a hug as soon as she steps through the door.

Love? Yes, I love her more than words can say. When did it happen? Actually, that day I first saw her and tried so hard not to care, love seeped through the barricades. You can't force love . . . but you can't stop it, either.

—Donna Sundblad

THE A-10 FIGHTER JET

"Guess what, class? Saturday, we're all going to the air force base to see a special movie and climb inside a big jet fighter plane. Won't that be fun!"

I grinned as I watched the six- and seven-year-olds' eyes grow wide and heard the raucous cheers that rattled the chairs in that little Sunday school room.

I couldn't help but feel a bit giddy at the thought of it all: My macho husband, Pete, sporting his gray-green flight suit with all the zippers and patches, would wow them with amazing facts about the A-10 "Warthog" fighter jet. They would *ooh* and *ahh* at the exciting, multichromatic, 8-millimeter movie. Then Pete, perched atop the super-duper aircraft, would usher them one by one into the cockpit, expound on the finer points of jet propulsion, and dazzle them with data on all the dials and instruments.

I was certain that by day's end, these awestruck kids would have had the thrill of a lifetime, telling their parents all about it using expressions such as "Wow!" and "Cool!" My expectations mounted through the week, until I actually envisioned the day they would tell their grandchildren about this, their "Most Memorable Moment."

Saturday morning arrived. I knew we were destined for trouble when Pete awoke with laryngitis.

"Oh no!" I shrieked. "Who will introduce the film? Who will sit in the cockpit as the children file up one by one? Who will point out all the instruments and answer all their questions?"

I was silly even to ask.

Before we knew it, the adventure was under way. Swarms of eager children and their equally excited parents filled one section of the small auditorium, while swarms of butterflies filled my stomach.

"Welcome," I began. "There's been a slight change . . ."

This was not how I'd planned it. At least I was confident that the movie would be a hit, because I'd previewed it two weeks earlier. Sitting down, I prepared to enjoy the nice little film about a sweet little airplane. Well, not exactly.

I didn't know that a new film had just replaced the one I had previewed. I sat in horror as music from *Jaws* pulsated, and the nose of the A-10 appeared over the horizon. Then, *k-a-b-o-o-o-o-m!* Screeching across the sky, this monster jet proceeded to blow up tanks, one by one, in living color, with the meanness of a killer shark and the decibel level of a bomb blast in the front row.

I caught the eye of one mother who had heard my rave reviews of the film. She glared. I winced.

After what seemed like a full-length saga, the reel finally ended and the lights came on. Stunned silence. I felt a sudden need to provide therapy along with the popcorn.

"Well now, let's go out to the airplane!" I scrambled to the door, thankful for the momentary reprieve and breath of fresh air.

Then, I spotted it. The monster tank-killer seemed to

gawk at me, daring me to climb aboard. Instinctively I looked behind me, hoping that everyone had run home. On the contrary, trailing behind me was a squad of squealing little people half my size, one-fifth my age, one-eighth of my formal education, and double my grit, counting on me to impart knowledge and lead them "to boldly go where no kid has gone before."

I felt responsible to fulfill their expectations.

Solemnly, I climbed the ladder of the plane, much like a French revolutionary soldier headed for the guillotine. Inside the cockpit, my job was to provide answers for these first and second graders' inquisitive young minds—answers to everything they had always wanted to know about fighter jets but were afraid to ask.

I scrunched into the snug leather seat and stared ahead. My eyes glazed over, bewildered by all the complex instruments, toggles and switches, assorted handles, levers, whirlimathings, and whatchamajigs. Surely, I would have to look these precious children in the eye and confess, "I know nothing, and I can prove it."

But God was gracious beyond words. Everything they wanted to know, I knew.

"This makes it go. This makes it stop. This is the microphone. No, there are no restrooms aboard. This is the eject handle. . . ."

That night, while my husband drifted off to sleep, I lay lost in thought. *Laryngitis . . . Switched movie . . . Alternate tour guide.*

"Not my Plan A," I sighed. "Seems nothing today went according to expectations."

Expectations? A familiar voice rang out from the past. *You won't always have control over these, Sandi. Hold them with an open hand.*

My mother's wise words always manage to tap me on the shoulder (or whack me on the side of my head) at the most fitting times.

She was right. I think back over the years, how expectations seemed to rule my life: I expected our family outings to top the charts in memorable experiences for our children. All our family devotions were destined to be rich in meaningful lessons. Our family reunions were certain to be packed with momentous moments and renewed relationships. Not wrong desires, but they are just that, desires.

God often does give us the desires of our hearts, and life seems good. But other times, he allows us to experience unexpected trials and troubles for our ultimate good, and life seems unfair.

> We foresee flawlessness. Life delivers brokenness.
>
> We plan perfection. Life makes other plans—it rains on our parades, dampening the spirits of those trying to march in step.
>
> We order a helping of idealism. Life serves up a plateful of reality. And reality bites. It ambushes us, hurling revised versions of our agendas our way, as we struggle to salvage the situation and reclaim some sense of stability.
>
> We organize a family outing. Inevitably, one of the kids gets a case of the flu.
>
> We look forward to a family reunion. Spoiled kinfolk spoil it.
>
> We try to teach our children about God. A case of the giggles develops during a deep devotional moment.

I'm finally "getting it," after much heartbreaking disappointment and self-imposed pressure: I need to expect the unexpected, to be flexible, to roll with the punches. Then, no matter what transpires, I'll be ready, and those around me will be relieved. Often those Plan B or even Plan W times turn out to be more fun, more memorable, and more rewarding than what had originally been planned, anyway.

It's been nearly thirty years since that Day of the Fighter Jet. Those six- and seven-year-olds now have kids of their own. I'm not sure about them, but as for me, I'm glad it worked out the way it did. I gained valuable insights, renewed perspectives, and a memorable story to tell to my grandchildren. Oh yes, and here's a footnote, free of charge, a wise admonition from Great-Grandmother about holding expectations with an open hand: Keep in mind Proverbs 19:21, which says, "You can make many plans, but the LORD's purpose will prevail."

—Sandi Banks

THE HANDWRITING ON THE TRANSFER TRUCK

"Honey, now don't panic, but I believe God is calling me to go back to school at Southeastern Seminary."

These were *not* the words a very pregnant mother of two boys, who had just settled into her newly remodeled home, wanted to hear.

Our family had recently moved back home to Georgia after spending four and a half years in Kentucky while my husband attended Bible college, followed by a missions assignment in Mississippi. Our two boys were born while Luke was in college, and I now rejoiced that our third son's arrival would be near friends, family, and grandparents who would undoubtedly be ecstatic to have a closer relationship with their grandsons. The bonus? Free babysitters, of course!

Adding to my bliss was the amazing house we had found, which we purchased with the help of at least two dozen miracles. It was the first home we had owned since well before college. I should also note that I cleaned and painted every surface in it myself. (OK, so maybe I had a *little* help.) I had come home in every sense of the word. The pregnancy nesting instinct intensified my need for a place to call my own in which to raise my little ones.

Have you seen the "Life Is Good" slogan? I believed it

and wore the T-shirt—that is, until the day of the I'm-going-to-seminary announcement.

"You've just got to be kidding me," was my not-so-spiritual, sarcastic reply. The rant continued with, "We can*not* move to North Carolina! We just got home! We just finished the house! We finally have something to call our own! You need to go back and talk to God again—I think some wires are crossed here. In fact, I am sure there's been a misunderstanding because he has not told me a thing!"

Looking back, even as I pitched my fit, I wasn't surprised. I can understand now that I had simply shut the door on the possibility of change because I was, in one dangerous word, *Content,* with a capital *C.*

This was a crisis of faith. "Why me? Why now? Why at all?" Nothing about the entire situation made any sense to me. My desperate prayers in those days were, "God, you are going to have to make this so clear to me that I can do nothing but acknowledge this is something you desire for us."

I trusted Luke's discernment on behalf of our family, but I had not yet heard the same confirmation from God that I had received in so many other situations before. When God had called us to attend Bible college, he spoke as clearly to me as he did to Luke. I was afraid but confident we were on the right path.

But this time Satan whispered, "Can you really trust Luke to hear on your behalf? Do you really believe God has your best interests at heart? It doesn't sound like he cares what this is doing to you."

It was truly enough to drive a girl to her knees. Thankfully, that is where I found my answer.

In my walk of faith, I have determined that God always

marks our paths with boulders and bread crumbs. The boulders are the huge things, the unmistakable signs of God's direction. We often see the bread crumbs, or what I have termed "God in the whispers," only in hindsight—after he has built our faith enough to recognize them. Looking back on this time in my life, I can now pick out the bread crumbs. But in those days, I needed a boulder. God did not disappoint me, and I think he even laughed a little in the process.

The "God, please convince me" prayer was one I whispered every minute of every day. I had given Luke a tentative, somewhat bitter, yes to the move but was still not convinced we were doing the right thing. We put the house on the market immediately so we could get moved before the fall semester began. It literally made me sick to my seven-months-pregnant stomach to drive by my home and have it proclaim, "For Sale"!

I left home one day (purposefully not looking at that dreaded sign) to run errands, and I distinctly remember praying, "God, you have just got to show me this is right."

On the day God answered my prayers, I had driven out of the subdivision with my kids in tow and traveled onto the highway. As I sped along, I noticed a transfer truck passing on my right. It immediately caught my eye because in large letters along the side it said, "Southeastern."

Hmm. This just happened to be the name of the seminary in question. But the tagline underneath stopped my breath because it read, "You've Made the RIGHT Decision."

Tears well in my eyes even now, years later, when I recall the shock at reading God's very personal answer to my constant prayers. I fully expected to pass that truck and see a winged messenger in the front seat, waving, smiling, and honking a horn loudly. My children were too young to recognize a "Praise you, Jesus" fit, but they saw one that day—staring wide eyed.

When I looked back on the experience, I was reminded of Scripture. "The apostles said to the Lord, 'Show us how to increase our faith'" (Luke 17:5). The disciples begged this of the Lord when he had just shared a standard of forgiveness they found impossible to uphold on their own. Jesus explained in the following verses how we are unworthy servants whose responsibility is simply to do what we ought to do.

Our role on planet Earth is to get ourselves ready while we are waiting for Christ's return. Only by faith in the One who desires wonderful things for us can we follow him, bread crumb by boulder, into the unknown. I can look now and realize seminary was part of the "what ought to be done" in our lives. It was a huge step in preparing for the ministry God had in store for our family. Though it was a difficult transition, I would not trade the wonders God revealed in our lives for a moment's comfort in the home I had so dearly loved.

We had confirmation of our decision quickly. First, my beloved house sold immediately, which meant we had the finances to move and start over in a new town. God gave me the grace to say good-bye, once again, and not make too much of a fool of myself in the process.

That was seven years ago. Now we live in Alabama—close enough to our hometown to still enjoy close grand-parent relationships and also have those blessed babysitters when we need them.

Second, Southeastern Freight Lines is a very common one in this part of the country. I see their trucks at least once a week. The tagline I read on every one of them is, "Quality Without Question." I've never seen another "You've Made the RIGHT Decision." I have often considered calling the truckline to ask about this, but I just don't think they would understand. I remain convinced it was a God-sized boulder, indeed.

"Lord, increase my faith!"

"Yes, child, just read the handwriting on the transfer truck."

—Lisa McKay

LOVE SONGS

My daughter Amelia and I huddled together in the front pew on the left side of the sanctuary. The church was packed for our combined Christmas morning service, which partly accounted for our sweaty palms. My daughter was to sing a solo in church. And whenever one of my daughters performs, she and I compete for the title "Most Nervous."

This solo was of particular concern to my daughter because she was fighting a nasty head cold. At almost eighteen, Amelia has been singing solos in church for fifteen years. However, her singing career has not been without incident so we always have plenty of reasons to worry. For instance, a solo sung at a school talent show when Amelia was in fifth grade comes to mind.

Amelia's tenth year of life had not been going well. That year we experienced a devastating family tragedy, which had many complicated and heart-wrenching aftereffects. One was that Amelia was suddenly estranged from her best friend at church, after five years of being as close as sisters.

Besides the lack of church friends, the girls at school were beginning to be catty and mean to one another. Even though Amelia was not one of their targets, she was getting weary of all the ugly behavior she witnessed day after day.

When we heard about the school talent show, I thought it would be a great diversion for us to concentrate on. We poured over song titles and finally agreed on the oldies tune "Put a Little Love in Your Heart."

Amelia practiced with the accompaniment tape for several weeks, and she handwrote all the lyrics on notebook paper to memorize.

The night of the talent show arrived. I dressed Amelia; her three-year-old sister, Lydia; and myself in matching red dresses as a sign of solidarity. Amelia's hair was brushed and styled to perfection. I thought we were as prepared as possible.

The school gym was full with performers and parents and siblings. For over an hour, I tolerated other children's skits, dances, and vocal ensembles. Knowing that Amelia was backstage having to wait so long made me a nervous wreck. I rocked Lydia back and forth, more for my benefit than hers. I accosted God with my silent pleas for him to remember all that Amelia had been through in the last few months and how she couldn't possibly handle anything remotely negative right now.

Suddenly, my little darling was standing alone on stage in front of a microphone. The introductory music began to play, and she began to sing her little heart out. She had sung about two lines beautifully when we heard an ugly and alien noise—the sound system was eating her background tape!

A look of sheer panic struck Amelia's face as her teacher encouraged her to sing a cappella. One brave-but-broken little entertainer fled behind the heavy curtains.

I rose to go comfort her when my husband's arm blocked my hasty departure. I gave him a look that said, "Don't mess with a maternal rescue mission." Slowly he opened his hand and revealed an extra accompaniment cassette tape. He said, with a mysterious smile, "A little voice told me to put it in my pocket for a possible emergency." I was too stunned to reply—I just grabbed the tape and ran, praying for help and wisdom.

Amelia, who rarely lets negative circumstances slow her down, felt humiliated. Even with another tape to try, she was mortified and, understandably, didn't want to go back out to face the crowd.

"I wouldn't go out there, but I know you can," I encouraged. "Just think of how hard you have worked for this and how badly you want to sing this song about love to these people. I don't want you to have any regrets. I believe in you, but you have to do this for yourself more than anything."

I'm not sure she believed me or agreed with anything I said, but being obedient and dutiful in nature, out she went. The audience of parents and grandparents was gracious and cheered her courage. The music began again, and as the song progressed, Amelia lost herself in the music and wowed her listeners. She completely captured her audience. As the song ended, the gym erupted in applause and a standing ovation that lasted several minutes.

Now, as we waited before another nerve-wracking solo, I felt blessed to have a memory of a magical moment. A Scripture came to mind and resonated in my spirit: "The LORD your God is living among you. He is a mighty savior. He will take delight in you with gladness. With his love, he will calm all your fears. He will rejoice over you with joyful songs" (Zephaniah 3:17).

I don't know why I often approach a new challenge with

fear and trepidation. Why would I be so worried and afraid that this would be the one big event that God wouldn't show up for? God is always faithful. Yet, somewhere in my humanity, I often think that maybe God doesn't care if my children or I fail or that I can't trust him to want happiness for us.

Today, God, I choose once again to believe in your grace and mercy, I prayed silently. *Prove yourself, once again, to be who you say you are for my daughter's sake.*

The pastor announced the offering. Amelia was to sing the offertory, so as she rose to the platform, I gave her hand one last squeeze. I held my breath as the instruments began to play. However, I soon let out a gasp and a sigh at the beauty of the melody. Amelia was singing a haunting rendition of the old Christmas carol "O Little Town of Bethlehem."

I had played it on the piano for her to practice at home dozens of times, but it sounded very different now. Our church pianist is a friend, and he had arranged the song in another key that was better for her vocal range. He had also written instrumental parts for a full orchestra, including a harp! There was my daughter—long curls framing a shining, angelic face, performing without effort or restraint with over six hundred witnesses to her God-given talent!

Tears streamed down my face as I realized how God was lavishing love on my daughter and me. What he was providing far exceeded anything I could have hoped for or imagined. It was as though he were actually speaking Ephesians 3:18-20, which says, "May you have the power to understand, as all God's people should, how wide, how long, how high, and how deep his love is. May you experience the love of Christ, though it is too great to understand fully. Then you will be made complete with all the fullness of life and power that comes from God. Now all glory to God, who is able, through his mighty power at work within us, to accomplish infinitely more than we might ask or think."

The cry and longing of my heart is that my daughters sense God's presence in their daily lives and that they will know he is continuously singing joyful songs over them. I also pray that my life will be a love song sung back to God and that others will hear and want to sing along.

—Evangeline Beals Gardner

THE GOD OF EXTREME MEASURES

"You're having your baby . . . tonight," the doctor said.

I couldn't believe my ears. We were still seven weeks from our due date. To induce my wife, Robin, that early seemed crazy.

Is this guy some sort of quack or something? I wondered.

"With blood pressure like that, Robin is a pressure cooker right now," he continued. "If we don't get the baby out of there, it will die."

DIE—there is a word you never want to hear from your doctor. It jolted me like I'd been hit with 240 volts. It took the breath out of me. I'm glad Robin wasn't close enough to hear our conversation.

"If we deliver the baby now, there is a reasonably good chance it will survive; if we don't, it won't. Either way, I'm not sure about Robin," the doctor said. He turned and went to make the necessary preparations for the delivery.

Not sure about Robin? I was stunned and turned toward Robin to see her panicked look. Lying on the hospital bed, she was already connected to a myriad of machines around her, whirring and beeping. Walking over to her, I considered what I was going to tell her. I didn't know what to say. My mind rapidly played back the tape of the last few minutes and hours.

We had enjoyed the pretty September day as we'd driven ninety miles from Uvalde, Texas, to San Antonio for Robin's regular OB visit. This had become routine, as we'd made this trek often. Because of our insurance, we were using a doctor and a hospital an hour and a half from our home.

Earlier in the pregnancy, Robin had been diagnosed with gestational diabetes, but that was under control now. Today, though, the doctor had other concerns—her blood pressure had gone up and stayed up. Nurses checked it several times, even having her lie on her side to help her heart work easier. Finally, her pressure did drop some.

Like a general commands a private, the doctor told me to get a blood pressure cuff immediately. While he gave instructions, warnings, and the list of the three things to watch for, I looked at our son, who was in the room with us. Sean was nine years old and had been to most of the doctor visits and had been to all of the sonograms with us. He had really taken ownership of this baby, for he had wanted a sibling for years.

We were thrilled that he was so interested. However, in this moment of warning, I could tell he was a bit anxious, as I was. When the doctor was on his way out of the office, he caught me in the hall and reiterated his instructions to get that cuff immediately and check Robin's blood pressure regularly.

We had a few errands to run before leaving town and heading home to Uvalde. I picked up a handy, battery-powered cuff as the doctor had advised, and then we stopped at a fast-food restaurant to eat. Robin just picked at her salad. When we left the restaurant, we sat in the car for a few moments. The visit with the doctor had been heavy, and Robin was upset, so I tried to keep the atmosphere light. I joked a little bit, and in the car in front of the restaurant, I tried the cuff on myself first. Yep, it worked fine.

Robin came next. Oh man, both numbers were higher than they had been in the doctor's office. I remembered that the doctor made her lie on her side and rest for a few minutes to bring down the blood pressure, so I tried this as well. It brought it down only a fraction.

What do I do? I thought a change of scenery might help, so off we went to run our errands. On the way to a baby store, I hit the button to recheck her pressure. Several minutes later, I did it again. Each time, the numbers got higher—much higher than the boundaries set by our doctor in his warning.

I knew then that we weren't going home that night, but I wasn't quite prepared for the night that we would face.

In front of the baby store, I tried the cuff one more time. Geez, higher still. I quickly got out of the car to go exchange the item we needed to replace, but Robin insisted that she go in. I tried to reason with her. Reason with a pregnant woman . . . what was I thinking? Robin insisted and finally told me that she was about to be sick. She ran inside the building and headed straight to the restroom.

That was strike three—she was out. Both numbers registering on the cuff were too high, and now she was vomiting. The doc's instructions were to call him if the bottom number exceeded a certain number or if the top number crossed a line or if Robin vomited. I was to call him if *only one* of the three happened. But now, all three had occurred in a matter of minutes. When I called the doctor, he instructed, "Get to the hospital right now. I'll meet you there."

Moments later, in the parking lot of the store, I knelt

to look Sean in the eyes. He looked afraid but was trying to be strong. I wondered what I should tell my little guy. I said we were taking Mommy to the hospital. As soon as the word *hospital* rolled out of my mouth, he cried, *"N-o-o-o-o-o!"* He, too, had understood the warnings in the doctor's office. He saw what was happening and recognized that this was a serious situation. By the time I calmed him down, Robin had returned, and we headed to the hospital.

Robin's blood pressure had skyrocketed even higher, so the doctor quickly took over that hospital wing and controlled everything like a general in a war zone. He managed the medical equipment, the staff, the room temperature, lighting, hall lighting, sounds . . . everything.

"You may lose her," he told me again. He was reasonably sure the baby would be fine, but things weren't looking very good for my bride of fourteen years.

For reassurance and advice, I called my sister, who is an operating-room nurse. Initially, she thought the doctor was overreacting to the gestational diabetes. Then, as I told her about Robin's blood pressure, she got quiet. She shocked me as she said in a very low, firm, and controlled voice, "Your doctor's right. The baby has to come right now."

By God's grace, we made it through that night. A friend picked up Sean during the evening, and Sarah Grace arrived the next day—healthy, but a little small. This child, who had had only thirty-three weeks in the womb, was whisked away to the neonatal intensive care unit (NICU) without either of us even touching her.

Thank goodness for digital cameras. Sarah Grace was in NICU, and Robin, because of complications, wasn't able to go to her. I ran back and forth taking pictures of Sarah and then showing them to Robin. By that afternoon, I was exhausted. Finally, I took a break and walked a couple of blocks to the Ronald McDonald House (RMH) to see about staying there for the next few weeks.

I didn't realize it, but I was a wreck. When I sat down in the RMH office, I said about three words to the person in charge, and then my voice stopped. A second later, I broke down and wept.

Sarah did great. Robin fared well too. Her recovery was a little slower than normal, but she got out of the hospital before Sarah did. Even at thirty-three weeks, Sarah wasn't as fragile as expected. Her lungs had developed, and her body worked as it should. When she reached five pounds and overcame her own complications, we all went home, with monitoring electronics in tow.

At home, we tried to process these happenings. We were so thankful. I relived those moments and conversations repeatedly, and I thanked God for such a positive outcome. We had a beautiful new daughter, and I still had my bride.

As I pondered all the events, something profound dawned on me. One of the first issues we had with this pregnancy was Robin's gestational diabetes. The test, with a zillion glasses of that nasty, chalky stuff, was only the beginning. With proper medication and diet, it became only a minor challenge. However, Robin worried about the side effects of diabetes in a pregnant woman. Diabetes significantly increases the baby's size. Robin hadn't been looking forward to delivering a large baby.

Typically, preemie babies struggle with lung issues, eye issues, digestive issues, and an assortment of other problems. We had none of these things to contend with—Sarah was healthy and fully developed. Why had these problems not happened with Sarah? And what happened to the other concerns we had before the blood-pressure issue took over?

Then it dawned on me. To a certain degree, Sarah wasn't early at all because she had developed faster than normal as a result of Robin's gestational diabetes. Now, here was my revelation: What we originally thought was a negative—an overdeveloped baby—was actually a positive. Perhaps God had developed the baby faster than normal because he knew the baby was coming early. In reality, the gestational diabetes was a good thing because it developed Sarah fast enough to be ready when the doctor ushered her into the world seven weeks early. Isn't God good?

Although I didn't enjoy the stress swarming around my girls' conditions during those critical weeks, I am so thankful for a loving God who took care of us—even through ways that we thought were bad. I learned to trust God more.

I've heard my whole life that "things aren't always what they seem." As a minister, I know and preach that we should continuously trust God. But I was worried. I was scared that I would lose one or both of my girls. This situation truly exemplifies where the rubber meets the road, to use an old cliché. My faith was being challenged. Oh, sure, I had faith in God, and I trusted him . . . but did I? Did I really trust him? Not until after the fact could I look back and see God's hand in all of it. At that point the pieces finally fit together, but what about when it was happening? Where was my faith then?

This was certainly a very special journey for me, for us. Sarah has grown to be such a big girl now. And the rest of us have grown to be more sensitive to God's mighty hand. Sean absolutely adores his little sister, Robin remembers very little of that night, and I have some very fond memories of how God saved my girls through extreme measures. I'm thankful that I serve a God whom I can trust.

—Dennis Stout

THE TRUE ADOPTION DAY

Our bouncing, blonde, blue-eyed, eighty-pound daughter arrived to join her sister and two brothers when she was eleven years old. I had been one of her sixth-grade teachers, and I had fallen in love with her.

She was in foster care and obviously needed lots of affection and stability. My husband and I had wanted a fourth child but had been advised, for health reasons, not to have another baby. Until we met Martha, we were content to put that dream aside. After prayer and serious family meetings, we started the adoption proceedings. She soon became a part of our family. We were amazed at how well Martha adjusted to her new surroundings, but she had had a lifetime of experience in adaptation.

Martha faintly remembered a baby sister who had been sitting in her high chair when the police came to take their mother to jail. By scrunching her eyes really tight and thinking hard, she could recall her mother's strawberry-blonde hair, but not much more. She had only fleeting, vague memories of her dad.

Our caseworker said, "She exhibits some behaviors of a child who has been abused. I believe if you adopt her and give her enough love, she can overcome her past and have a happy future."

After he explained adoption to Martha, he asked her, "Do you want to have your parents' rights terminated? Do you want to be adopted and have a real, forever home?"

She eagerly and bravely answered, "Yes, I do."

The process to make her legally ours dragged on for two years.

We knew a little about her background. Martha's father had abandoned the family when Martha was three. After her mother was taken away, her baby sister was adopted quickly by a family that had helped care for the sisters. Martha, however, then lived with her dad, usually in an old, beat-up car. One time, during their wanderings, he accepted help from a church. People there had said, "If you ever need us again, come back." He did, leaving his little girl with them, never to return for her.

An agency placed Martha with three different foster families, but she never had a sense of belonging. In at least one home, she suffered unjust "punishment."

Just as she would settle in to another new home, the family's needs or circumstances would change. They would pack her bags and toys, and she would move on to a new family. She learned to never look back—to just close off that part of her life as if it had never happened.

After those foster homes, where she had been the only child in custodial care, she was placed in a large-group foster home. She stayed there four years, and this environment provided more stability than she had previously felt. Unfortunately, she was the only young child living there. The other residents were teenagers, who taught her more than a child should learn.

Soon after she came to live with us, a job transfer took us fifteen hundred miles away. We encouraged her to stay in contact with her last foster family because they had treated her like one of their own children and had even considered adopting her. But Martha didn't want to stay in touch. That chapter in her book of life was firmly closed, and she was ready to start over again.

"Lord, help us know what to do, to say, to help her heal and grow into healthy womanhood," we prayed as we committed our hearts to a lifetime of love for her. The way was often rocky.

Back then she would hopefully ask, "Mom, do you love me as much as you love my sister and brothers?"

I would reassure her, "Yes, I do. Love comes from caring for children, not just from bearing them. And love lasts forever." She would smile and be content for a while.

Thinking it might help, I told her one day that I understood a little about being adopted. "I am adopted too," I said. Her eyes grew even wider when I explained I was the adopted child of a king! Then I read from my Bible, "God decided in advance to adopt us into his own family" (Ephesians 1:5).

"I had to voluntarily accept God as my Father," I said, "kind of like you had to accept us as your parents. When I was adopted, I inherited a lot of brothers and sisters, too, and God loves all of us the same. His love is forever."

I wasn't sure she understood that concept, but it seemed to help. She still hovered near, always wanting to sit next to me and hold my hand. Martha was perfectly behaved, pathetically eager to please, and willing to do more than her share of chores. The problem was, as I learned, that it was Martha's way of trying to earn our love.

Again and again she would ask for reassurance of our love, but she never dared test it.

I tried to help her see that being perfect is not a requirement of being loved. "When I make mistakes, God doesn't stop loving me. I am still his child," I explained. I knew it would be easy for Martha to grow up blaming God or herself for her past.

I prayed she would be able to relate to the things I said. I wanted her to understand unconditional love and discipline. The words of Hebrews 12:6 came to mind: "The LORD disciplines those he loves, and he punishes each one he accepts as his child."

I told her I believed that when bad things happened in my life, they didn't happen because God caused them to happen. "He helped me get through those hard times," I said. "And that disciplined me to grow stronger and depend on him."

She seemed to understand a lot for an eleven-year-old child; however, she still continued to model exemplary behavior and still needed verbal assurance that we loved her.

"I guess it will just take a lot more time and a lot of love for her to feel safe enough to misbehave," I reasoned.

Little did I know that Martha was poised to speed up that process. The day soon came when she flagrantly disobeyed me while riding home from the grocery store.

"Yippee!" I inwardly screamed, but at the same time, I knew she needed stern discipline.

I was shaking when we got out of the car. The other children looked at each other and then at me. I could almost read their thoughts, *What is Mom going to do? We couldn't get away with that.*

Martha just sort of grinned while she stubbornly stared me down.

She had bravely drawn a line in the sand. I gulped and

crossed over it. "Young lady, go to your room, *now.*" I hurt all over and was in sheer agony as I went inside to discipline her.

I was not prepared for her response. She threw her little arms around my neck, face glowing.

"Thanks, Mom," she gushed. "Now I feel real!"

That day became her true adoption day.

—Elaine Young McGuire

CHILD'S PLAY

When my two sons were preschoolers, complete strangers would ask me, "Are they yours?"

People who knew me a little better would say, "It's hard to believe a low-key person like you could have such rambunctious kids."

Those close to me spoke more bluntly. My younger brother called them "the wrecking crew." My sophisticated (and childless) boss called them "the worst case scenario." My husband and I agreed that if we could harness the boys' energy, we'd save a bundle on utility bills.

They ran full tilt every waking moment, but they were absolutely devoted to each other. If my four-year-old wanted to build an igloo, my two-year-old would help him carry the ice cube trays into their bedroom and supervise the project. If my two-year-old decided to see how many times he could jump between the sofa and the armchair, my four-year-old happily counted for him.

A typical day began at 5:00 A.M. with the insistent jangle of an old-fashioned alarm clock. We put the clock in the boys' room to keep them in bed, not to wake them up. They had paper and crayons for quiet play until the alarm went off—sometimes they'd fill up three or four pages with busy scribbles by the time I went in for good-morning hugs.

When the alarm stopped, "Round One," as my husband called it, began. Getting the boys dressed wasn't exactly a knock-down, drag-out fight but rather more like a tag-team match. Between streaking stark naked to the toilet and wriggling under the bed to find favorite socks, they always worked up a good appetite for breakfast.

We lived on the third floor of a large apartment building in Southern California at the time. It had one unreliable elevator, and getting up and down the stairs with the kids, the stroller, and various toys was a major operation. I limited trips outside by combining visits to the park or the beach with chores such as grocery shopping or doing the laundry.

To compensate for the lack of outdoor play space, we turned our living room into a rumpus room. We had a swing attached to a door frame and a plastic slide and even a small trampoline. The boys kept all their toys there, and we picked them up only once a week. Our downstairs neighbor left for work around 8:00 each morning. Until he came home, the boys could romp and play as they pleased. I kept an eye on them as I did chores, awestruck by their unquenchable energy.

At times, I enjoyed their high jinks, like those mother bears you see in the nature documentaries lumbering around looking for honey while their cubs tumble and tussle nearby and get into mischief. Other times, their perpetual motion reduced me to the lonely desperation known only to the mothers of preschoolers. Then I'd turn to the Bible for guidance. I found special consolation in Matthew 18:3: "I tell you the truth, unless you turn from your sins and become like little children, you will never get into the Kingdom of Heaven."

One particularly frantic day, I could find no relief for the stress of containing two little dynamos in one cluttered room. I strapped my two-year-old into his stroller and stuffed shoes onto my four-year-old's feet.

"We're going to the beach!" I barked. Of course, the elevator was out of order. As we tromped down the concrete stairs, the boys picked up on my grim mood. We marched silently for six blocks under a winter sky as cold and gray as metal all the way to the beach.

I set up "camp" by one of the lifeguard stations and watched the two of them frolic on the wide stretch of sand. Always mobbed on weekends, the place seemed eerily deserted on this weekday. I scolded myself for bringing the boys here on such a dreary day, but they didn't seem to mind. My older son drew life-size pictures of construction equipment, his current passion, in the sand with a stick. His little brother toddled around gathering as many shells as his chubby little fists could hold.

Seeing how they took such pleasure in simple things helped me unwind a little. I knew the drawings would disappear by morning and the shells would be lost before we got halfway home. Still, I felt grateful for the fresh air and the open space for the children to run and play.

Sand scraped against wood in the lifeguard chair above my head. I looked up to see a man in ragged clothes climbing down from the elevated platform. Why hadn't I noticed him earlier? Instinctively, I jumped up to position myself between him and my children. Both of them smiled at the man, and the little one waved and shouted, "Hi, there!"

The man walked over to me, his legs stiff from crouching in the chair. He smelled like a dumpster but bowed formally before he spoke. "Are you born in Christ's love?" he asked in a strange accent.

As a longtime, big-city resident, I sensed a clever come-on. If I said yes, he'd hit me up for money. Ignoring his kind, sad eyes, I said no.

He pulled out an index card that had been torn and repaired so many times it was completely covered with tape. He handled the ratty piece of paper reverently, and part of me wondered what it would be like to cherish something that much. He looked at me solemnly and said, "Repeat after me."

I decided it would be better to humor him. He might be emotionally unstable, and if he started yelling, he'd scare the boys. So I repeated his words, accepting Jesus Christ as my Savior and asking forgiveness for my sins.

As I spoke, the child in me remembered the Bible story of Jesus finding disciples on a beach and how they followed him with no questions asked.

To my surprise, the man quickly pocketed his card when he was done reading and grasped my shoulders. Then he kissed me on both cheeks the way they do in French movies. "God bless us all," he said and walked away.

I'd never felt so ridiculous in my life—letting a stranger, and a smelly one at that, kiss me. What kind of example was I setting for my sons with this irresponsible behavior? My grown-up self argued that this freakish encounter had nothing to do with true Christian faith.

Behind me, the boys clapped and cheered. Turning to them, I couldn't deny the feeling that a heavy weight had been lifted from my heart. The joy in their faces charged me with new understanding of how immediate Christian faith can be. As simple as a smile, as quick as a giggle, Christ's love embraces the childlike heart with no strings attached.

I ran to the boys and caught them up in a silly game we called tickle-tag. My enthusiasm more than matched theirs as I scrambled on my hands and knees, chasing after them, looking for a chance to tickle. We all ended up sprawled in the sand, laughing hysterically. Our dreary day at the beach had become a wild and crazy adventure.

At dinner that night, my husband asked our older son how his day had been. He said, "We had a great time. We went to the beach, and Mommy kissed the lifeguard twice."

I explained the whole thing in detail to my flabbergasted husband, but to this day, I don't think he believes me.

—Vivian Reed

ANSWERED PRAYER IN JAMAICA

Traveling to do TV specials has always been a very important aspect of my job as a television talk show host. One of my most challenging trips was when our TV crew, consisting of me and my husband and our cameraman and his wife, went to Jamaica.

A Jamaican plantation owner, Jack Wilmont, had paid all our expenses so we could do a TV feature on his operation. While we were there, we also planned to do a documentary on a Jamaican orphanage run by an American preacher and his wife.

The flight from America to Jamaica was pleasant, but everything changed the minute we touched down in Montego Bay. Going through customs was a disaster. The preacher had apparently failed to get a permit to allow our TV equipment to be admitted into the country. We also realized the inspector wanted a bribe. I was determined not to pay him anything, no matter what. So, we did what we always do in an emergency—we prayed.

In a few minutes, I walked back to the customs counter. A second man had joined the man who had been giving us such a hard time.

I smiled, and in my most pleasant voice I said, "Look,

we had no idea our hosts had not made arrangements for our TV equipment to be admitted."

One of the customs agents had told us we couldn't take our camera in because of the black market. He said we might be trying to sell this equipment inside Jamaica illegally.

"We are here to do two television specials," I explained. "Jack Wilmont has paid our expenses to come here, and besides, you can keep us in Jamaica if we don't have our television equipment when we start for home!"

The two men looked at each other, and the new man said, "OK, lady," and stamped our papers. I was elated! Either God had given me just the right words or the name Jack Wilmont had changed their minds. Whatever the case, we were on our way.

Just outside the terminal, we met our next challenge. The preacher who ran the orphanage met us. He had rented a tiny, two-door Volkswagen to carry us to our destination. It took an hour to tie our equipment, suitcases, and other belongings on top of the car. All four of us squeezed into the car with the preacher and held our breath.

He took off in a spin, talking and laughing as he went. We kept looking at each other as he sped through town and headed for the mountains.

"Slow down!" I finally exclaimed. "You'll have a wreck!"

"Oh, no," he assured us. "There is no speed limit in Jamaica. Everyone drives like this."

"I don't care!" I said. "If we lose that equipment, our boss will never forgive us!"

He slowed down just a little, but as he headed up into the hills, he sped up again.

"Where are we going?" I finally asked.

"Just wait and see," he smiled. "Have we got a surprise for you!"

Did he ever have a surprise for us! When we arrived at our accommodations, we were in a state of shock. The front door of a simple block house opened, and out came ten adorable little Jamaican children. They clapped, sang, and waved their greeting to us. Our hearts melted.

Yes, we were to spend our time in Jamaica at the orphanage. We had no air conditioning and no hot water. My husband and I slept on a three-quarter bed. The cameraman and his wife slept on bunk beds. Although the weather was very hot and humid, the water piped down from a mountain stream was ice cold. The soap never lathered either. When any of us showered, we squealed.

However, getting to know the children was worth the inconveniences. If we could have, we would have loaded them up and brought them home with us.

The next morning, we headed for Jack Wilmont's plantation. On the way, we went through Fern Gully, a beautiful passageway through lush, green foliage. However, our route led us on a continuous drive that went round and round and round. We were crowded in that tiny Volkswagen. There was no air conditioning, and as we went round and round, we all began to get sick. We had to stop to try to get back our equilibrium. The cameraman, Wayne, threw up continually and was very dizzy. What could we do? We had to do the television documentary with the man who had paid for our trip. But Wayne was so sick. We couldn't do the documentary without him. Again, we prayed.

Soon, Wayne was able to get back into the car. We had to drive slowly but soon arrived at the plantation. Wayne had to lie down, while the rest of us were treated to the best meal we had eaten all week.

The Wilmont plantation consisted of a thriving restaurant, a Jamaican zoo, and an amazing farm. The family home was perched on the side of a mountain, with a huge Olympic-sized pool overlooking the farming operations. After our meal, we enjoyed a guided tour through the entire plantation.

Wayne was still trying to get well enough to do his camera work. It seemed impossible. Jerome, my husband, was a good still photographer, but he knew nothing about a video camera. We continued to pray. Finally, Wayne was able to set up the camera with my husband's assistance. With God's help, we did the taping. Jack was a kindly host. His wife was an elegant Jamaican lady who carried herself like a princess. Visiting the Wilmont complex was an adventure we'll never forget. Then we set off for the long trip back to the orphanage.

When we finished our taping, it was time to go home. We insisted that the preacher take us to Montego Bay the night before our flight, so we could sleep at a hotel and get to the airport quickly the next day. When we arrived at the hotel, only one room was available. We took it! We were so thankful that there were two double beds in the room.

We didn't sleep much that night because we were all laughing and talking about the many crazy things that had happened during the trip.

The next morning we had to go through customs again. Could we get our television equipment home? That was the big question. We prayed. A different man was at the counter. He hesitated momentarily, and then he stamped our papers. We almost ran to the plane.

When we got back home, America had never looked better to us. The first place we stopped after we landed was at a restaurant. Food had never tasted so good either—we'd lived mainly on peanut butter at the orphanage. The four of us agreed that the farthest place south we'd travel for a while would be Florida.

However, through our adventures, we were able to produce a documentary that helped those orphaned children get much-needed financial help. And we learned that no matter what we faced, God was always there to hear and answer our prayers. Thankfully we learned the truth of Psalm 34:4: "I prayed to the LORD, and he answered me. He freed me from all my fears."

—Ann Varnum

HOW MARGE TAUGHT ME GRATITUDE

I never knew her last name. She was just Marge, the cafeteria gofer—"go fer" this, "go fer" that. She cut pies and chopped lettuce and was generally low woman on the totem pole.

On this especially busy day, she was assigned to help me. I was the cafeteria's head baker. Making small talk as we stemmed fresh strawberries for pies, I asked, "Any kids, Marge?"

"Nine."

"Nine?"

"Nine." Five by her first husband, four by her second. *Probably too many kids, too little money, and likely a couple of divorces,* I thought. But no, as we cleaned the strawberries, she said something about "when my first husband died." Later she mentioned, "when my second husband died."

Somehow the conversation drifted to church. I commented that the thing I disliked about the restaurant business was working on Sundays. Marge said, "Me, too. I send the kids and wish I could go myself. But the Lord's been so good to me."

I thought her spirit of gratitude and loving God was incredible for a woman who had been widowed twice and left with nine kids. I couldn't help but ask, "How's that, Marge?"

"Oh, what he did for me when my second husband died!" Then she told me that when her husband had terminal cancer, their insurance ran out. They first sold their camper, then their boat, later the cars to pay doctor, hospital, and drug bills. Eventually, they had to sell their house. Then they moved into what Marge called a "rent house."

Her husband had to be hospitalized repeatedly. She said, "The bills ran up, and we finally ran out of money and had nothing left to sell."

When there was nothing else the hospital or doctors could do to help him, Marge took her husband home to the "rent house"—to die. But the need for painkillers and medication continued. She said that one day the drugstore told her the bill was so large she couldn't fill any more prescriptions on credit.

A man from Marge's church owned a bakery. When he heard about Marge's financial helplessness, he told her, "Marge, I can't give you the money you need, but I can give you a job and all the overtime you can work."

So she went to work putting bread dough in loaf pans.

"Jim, I don't know how many ninety- to one-hundred-hour weeks I put in," she said. "I got so tired I was afraid I'd fall asleep on my feet and they'd have to fire me." She laughed. "The circulation in my feet got so bad standing all those hours that all my toenails turned black and fell off.

"But finally it ended. One of my neighbors had been looking in on my husband for me while I worked. She called one day and said, 'Marge, you need to come right away.'"

Marge continued talking to me, "Now, Jim, when I married the second time, my youngest child, a girl, was only a baby. Her stepdaddy was the only daddy she ever knew—and how she loved her daddy!"

That daughter came home after school each day, cleaned up her stepfather, and took care of him.

"She was a real trooper," Marge said, "but my great fear was that she'd come home from school one day and find her daddy dead. So I prayed, 'Dear Lord, don't let that happen.' I don't believe after all she'd been through she could have taken that.

"When I reached the house that day, the screen door was propped open and the ambulance was backed up to the door. As I started in, the driver, who'd been there several times, shook his head and said, 'He's not hurting anymore, Marge.'

"Though I had known for months this time was coming, I still had to cry. As I turned away from the door, I saw my daughter coming up the walk from school, and I thought, *Oh Lord, thank you. You answered my prayer.*"

She said, "Jim, God saw that I was there when my daughter needed me. He's been so good to me."

Marge's words spoke to me not just that day, but replayed in my mind for days, months, and years—even still today.

Marge's gratitude to God when her husband had just died has become a parable for me. Her story changed how I see people in the world about me and the assumptions I tend to make about them. Too many times I'm like Abraham. When the king of Gerar asked why he had passed off Sarah as his sister instead of his wife, Abraham replied, "I thought, 'This is a godless place'" (Genesis 20:11). Too often, I assume that I know people's spiritual condition.

Marge was working to support a big family by herself. She seldom got to church. Yet, somehow, in spite of hardship, heartbreak, and death, she maintained her faith in God. She trusted that he not only was "Someone up there" but also knew what she was struggling with down here. She had faith and confidence that God cared and was involved in how things turned out for her, for her dying husband, and for her vulnerable daughter.

Faced with death, debt, and family demands, Marge was thankful that she was at the right place at the right time. God made sure she was there when her daughter needed her mom. She understood what Paul meant by telling us to "be thankful in all circumstances" (1 Thessalonians 5:18).

And, thanks to Marge, when I face tough times in my own life, I remember to be thankful too.

—Jim Rawdon

ALICE

The auditorium of the old elementary school was silent. The omnipresent smell of busy children blended with the musty fragrance of old tennis shoes. Wooden folding chairs were arranged two feet apart in three rows on the stage. Metal collapsible music stands stood waiting for sheets of music.

I shook my head in dismay, remembering a recent sword fight between two of my students. It had resulted in more stands being sent to the "Of No Use" box at the back of the stage, which held contents the art teacher would later use.

"These are perfect for my next venture into modern sculpture," she had said, a spark of enthusiasm in her eyes.

After taking a final look at my lesson plan, I heard the class approaching. The auditorium doors swung open, and the students hurried in with their violin and viola cases.

"Come, children, take your places. First row, line up to be tuned. The rest of you rosin your bows and study your notes. We'll start with our D major scale and then work on 'Jingle Bells.'"

"But it's not even Thanksgiving," yelled one boy from the back of the stage. "Don't you know any Thanksgiving songs?"

"Class, I do know some Thanksgiving songs, but we aren't quite ready for that caliber of music."

"What's a caliber?" asked a soft voice.

Without looking, I knew who spoke. It was Alice, a timid girl with long, auburn hair and azure eyes. She always had a pleasant smile on her face when she came to have her violin tuned. If I had a favorite of the more than a hundred students at five elementary schools, it would be Alice. She took instruction well and had a natural ear for playing the violin. The child also had a maturity beyond her ten years.

The rest of the class laughed at Alice for asking the question. Her face turned as red as the old, worn curtains hanging on both sides of the stage.

"That's a good question. Would anyone like to define *caliber*?" A hush fell over the auditorium.

"Well, girls and boys, it has to do with quality. I use the term in the sense that it would be difficult for us to learn a Thanksgiving song. After all, we just started to read notes. We need to spend our time preparing for our Christmas program. Perhaps next year we'll learn a Thanksgiving piece."

Soon, the squeaky sounds of beginning violin students filled the air. The custodian sweeping in the back of the auditorium winced at the noise of the children playing their instruments. He put his broom aside and left.

I didn't mind the sound—I reflected on my own early attempts.

As usual, the class time passed quickly. A bell rang, signaling the end of the period. The string students lost no time putting their instruments away, for it was lunch time.

"Don't forget to stack the chairs to the left side and put the stands over in the corner. No one is to leave until the stage is clear."

I hurried to stack music and gather my belongings.

I muttered, "Just enough time to eat lunch in the car and get to my next school."

As I turned to check the empty stage, I was surprised to see Alice standing a few feet away.

"My goodness, you startled me, Alice."

Her eyes welled with tears, and the vibrant color in her face turned to ashen white. "Can I show you something?"

"Of course. What is it?"

The child hung her head. With trembling hands, Alice lifted her blouse to show her midriff. Ugly bruises covered her skin. She pulled down her jeans a little to show the same marks on her stomach.

"My goodness, Alice. How did that happen?"

"My mother did it," she whispered.

The girl choked on her tears, picked up her violin case, and ran out of the auditorium. I stood rooted to the spot, shaking my head in disbelief. How could a mother do such a thing?

I immediately went to the school nurse and reported the incident.

"What can I do?" I asked.

The school nurse said, "We have cases like this all the time. I'll take care of it from here. Nothing for you to worry about."

The weekend passed slowly. My thoughts and prayers often returned to Alice. Usually Monday morning arrived much too soon, but not this time.

When I returned to the school, I paced back and forth, waiting for my string class to arrive. But Alice didn't come. Perhaps her teacher had held her back for makeup work, or perhaps she was absent. I could no longer stand the suspense.

"Class, where is Alice today?"

"She's transferred to another school," a student explained.

My heart sank. What would become of her? Was she safe? Did her mother take her away?

After class I discovered that Alice had been sent to live with her father. That was the only information I could get. I lost all contact with her. I felt so helpless. If only I had spoken more to Alice that day. If only . . .

For some reason the thought of the child tugged at my heart. Perhaps Alice reminded me of myself as a child. I was also quite shy, and my music was an important part of my youth.

Years passed. Now and again I would see a girl who reminded me of Alice. Tears would fill my eyes, and a prayer for Alice would explode in my heart.

One Saturday morning I had to go shopping. *I detest the mall on Saturdays,* I thought. *All those rude teenagers and their loud music.*

Dodging through the crowds, I heard someone call my name. I turned to see three teenage girls in high school letter jackets walking my way.

"Don't you remember me? I'm Alice. I was in your string class at Roosevelt Elementary."

For a few moments I stared at the lovely young girl standing in front of me. I couldn't believe my eyes. She still had that loving, gentle look about her.

"Of course I remember you. I've thought of you often and wondered how you were getting along."

Alice understood the unasked question.

"I've been with my father and stepmother since I left."

Alice held out the sleeve of her red and blue letter

jacket. "And see, I lettered in band and got a first place in the regional contest on flute. I was ahead of all the others in my class because of my violin lessons."

"Come on, Alice. We'll be late to meet everyone at McDonald's," said one of her impatient friends.

"Guess I better go. Good to see you again."

"Good to see you again, too, Alice."

I watched the girls walk away until they were lost in the crowd. My eyes teared in grateful appreciation as I prayed a quiet "Thank you."

As a teacher, I've learned through the years that my influence may be strong in others' lives, but it is still limited. Thankfully, as with Alice, when we can't be there to look after the ones we care for, we can commit them to God's care. He protects those we love, shepherding them and guiding them—after all, he cares for them even more than we do!

—Emily Tipton Williams

FEAR FACTOR

As we gazed from the mountaintop deep in the lush green forests of rural China, we saw an amazing panorama. From base to peak—just like tiers of a wedding cake—hundreds of rice paddies filled the hillsides. The rice paddies are the livelihood of the Dong people who live there. *Dong* means "hidden," and their wooden villages are truly hidden in the crooks and shadows of these mountains.

This scene before me was beyond anything I could imagine. And yet just weeks before, my fear of coming here had been beyond anything I could imagine. I can't remember when I've been that terrifed.

When my pastor had first called to ask if I'd consider going to China with a group of high school kids to visit missionaries and "prayer walk" through villages, I was exhilarated because the thought of going to China was like one of those "extreme" shows. The idea sounded really cool.

Pop went those fantasy balloons. That first adrenaline rush evaporated, and a deep, dark fear of the unknown set in fast.

As news kept coming about the trip, my fear increased. "Pack everything in waterproof bags, or rain could soak everything." "Bring some of your own food, as we're not certain where every meal will come from." "You can bring only a carry-on bag, no other luggage!"

I was going to the other side of the world, to a remote people group in the mountains of China to visit people who don't even have a written language yet. How does one pack for that? I can barely pack in one carry-on for a weekend in town! I'm known as the one who packs everything I could ever need plus everything anyone else could ever need.

"Oh, and bring a bedroll," they told us. "We might have to sleep on plywood." I'm not used to roughing it. When I was a kid, camping was traveling around in an Airstream trailer where we baked cookies at night and my parents had a king-size bed. I didn't rough it. For someone who plans for every detail, this was a nightmare. How do I prepare for something that I know nothing about?

But the more frightened I got, the more I prayed. This drove me into the arms of my heavenly Father at breakneck speed. I was like a scared child with arms outstretched, running and slamming into his or her parents and clutching them for dear life.

I tried desperately to think of good reasons not to go. But I really didn't have any. Even most of the cost was taken care of by the church because another adult was needed to chaperone.

The unknown loomed before me, coming closer and closer—a dark chasm with no answers. The Lord had seen me through unknowns before. My husband had started having heart problems at the age of thirty-four. There were times I'd wake up to make sure he was still breathing. At the age of four, my son started having seizures and was diagnosed with epilepsy—another trip to the wasteland of worry. The Lord was with me through all of those situations. Why would he abandon me now?

I knew God was asking me to trust him and go, that there was no way I could look him in the face and say no and slink away. I had to trust him and jump into the chasm.

It drove me to him, just as David described in Psalm 42:1: "As the deer longs for streams of water, so I long for you, O God." I longed for the Lord. I read verses, wrote verses, prayed verses, and memorized verses. I was hungry for his sustenance because I knew he was all I would have. I would leave my comfortable routine, my home, and my country. In China I wouldn't be known as a mom or a wife. I would just be me. So I clung to him.

My anxiety came to a head when we were at the airport and I started to walk onto the plane. My heart was pounding wildly, I could hardly breathe, and a flood of tears was about to break as I waved to my family. My husband stood with my two young daughters by his side, half hidden, crying. They could not understand why their mommy would go somewhere so far away and leave them. *This is it—there's no turning back now,* I thought. I was shaking.

When I sat down, I wasn't next to anyone on my team. I was alone. I almost lost it, but the gentleman next to me interrupted my hyperventilation and asked where I was going. I started to tell him. He was enthralled. He has no idea how his rapt attention gave me what I needed to make it through that flight.

God is faithful, so faithful! Why do I not learn? After we'd flown to California and then to Seoul, Korea, my fear flew away! The shadow that had plagued me and poisoned me for weeks was gone.

I had experienced the unknown in many other areas,

and God had brought me through each one. Why had I not trusted him with this one? I thought of the scene from the Disney movie *Aladdin,* in which Aladdin on his magic carpet holds out his hand to the princess and asks, "Do you trust me?" Christ reached out his hand to me and asked, "Do you trust me to take you on a magic carpet ride to China?"

I thank the Lord I took his hand because he gave me the ride of my life. I'd stepped into a world I'd known only through picture books, Sunday night missionary slides, and TV documentaries.

We ended up in a place where time has stood still. People have farmed rice here the same way for hundreds of years. They sow each plant by hand. Standing ankle deep in water and mud, with their pants rolled up and straw hats to shade them, they precisely put each plant into the water, row after row, hour after hour, and generation after generation. They harvest and plow their fields just as their forebears did—with a water buffalo and a wooden yoke and plow.

As I watched them working their rice paddies in the heat of the day, Christ's words in Matthew 11:28-29 became a living picture before me: "Come to me, all of you who are weary and carry heavy burdens, and I will give you rest. Take my yoke upon you. Let me teach you, because I am humble and gentle at heart, and you will find rest for your souls."

They would understand these words in a way I never could. I felt as if I were looking through Christ's eyes as he watched the people work the land more than two thousand years earlier, saw their burden, and had great compassion on them in their misery.

One day as we walked through a village, we stopped to rest on a small, intricately painted bridge. Above me were ancient renderings of mystical legends and spiritual myths. Under my feet were thousands of smooth stones embedded very carefully and artistically turned this way and that. When the people came down from their rice fields, they took off their sandals and walked back and forth across them. These stones, researchers have discovered, lowered blood pressure and improved balance. The water that ran below me was full of sewage; even so, women squatted on rocks scrubbing clothes.

I glanced up as a very old woman hobbled to the bridge. The lines of age, hard work, and sun were etched across her face. She had a crooked walking stick and was completely bent over. She took a seat across from me on the bridge, and our eyes met. It was an unforgettable moment to look in her eyes and have our worlds collide. *If only I could see what her eyes have seen and understand the burdens her withered frame has carried. Oh, how priceless it would be to sit at her feet and hear the truly amazing stories she could tell. Yet, Lord, you know her well, every need and every ache—you know them all. You know all her thoughts.* I realized that God speaks Dong.

One day as I stood on a road that overlooked a Dong village, I prayed that we would be a great light that would cause wonder. I prayed that somehow our trip would cause a stirring in people's souls, an awakening, a quickening in their spirits. I prayed that something would "shift" when we were there that could point only to God.

As we prayed for them, across the Pacific thousands of miles away from us, others prayed for us. Mothers and fathers, sisters and brothers, loved ones and friends—hearts were interceding for us. God heard those prayers and stirred into action for us as well.

"What did you do in China?" people ask me.

We prayed.

"You didn't build anything or bring them anything?"

No, we just prayed. And two years later my husband arrived in China and walked the same villages. The missionary told my husband's group that he now knows of one Christian in each village. Out of 2.5 million Dong people, it's estimated there were only 1,500 Christians—now there are 1,508.

My prayer walk through China has forever changed me. I will never look at the news of other countries and the plight of their people the same way. I will never look at another person from China the same way. You have a kinship, a bond that is created with other people when you've walked their dusty roads, when you've eaten from their bowls, when your eyes have met and you've wondered about one another's worlds, and when you've lived among them. Their world invades your being, in a way pictures never will. For me to have had a glimpse into lives from another world was a priceless gift.

Oh, what I would have missed! I wonder how many other "gifts" God has carefully chosen, gift wrapped with a handwritten note, and handed to me with great anticipation only for me to push them aside. If someone would have told me that one day I would travel into the heart of China, I would have suspected they missed the Just Say No to drugs campaign.

Never say never. A missions trip, no matter how near or far, could be one of the most amazing gifts that God is anxiously waiting to give you. Maybe there's a magic carpet with your name on it, and he's reaching down to you asking, "Do you trust me?"

—Tamara Vermeer

THE NEW PERFUME

Two tiny skunk kittens peeked around the flowerpots stored in the shed.

"Oh, there you are, sweeties!" I said. "Where's number three?"

The temporary cage was empty. I set down the canned cat food. My husband, a wildlife biologist, had asked me to feed the baby skunks before I left for work because he had an early meeting. The kittens were to be transferred to a nice wilderness home on the wildlife management area that evening. Collected from under a trailer late the night before, the skunks were just old enough to be on their own.

I loved helping with the variety of baby wild critters that my husband occasionally brought home. We were a bed-and-breakfast for fawns, young hawks, raccoon cubs, boar piglets, and even bear cubs. This was the first time I was so close to baby skunks, and they were adorable.

I thought about my morning list: shower, devotions, breakfast, make lunches, iron uniform, put cat outside. I realized I had enough time to search for the escapee. Careful not to smudge my uniform, I slid on some work gloves and pushed aside the dog food buckets. The shed floor had holes large enough for the skunks to get out—and I didn't want them to take up residence under our old farmhouse or tangle with the cat or the coonhounds out back.

Number three tiptoed from behind the lawnmower. He looked like a stuffed toy. "Oh, you are so swe-e-e-e-t," I told him as I approached.

Unimpressed, the kitten turned away and stomped his tiny back feet. A matchstick tail curled up. His act was better than a cartoon. I wondered if I had time to find the camera. What a great calendar shot.

A small *p-s-s-s-t* sound came from his nether region. He pretended to let me have it. How cute! Laughing, I told him, "Oh, you're too tiny to smell!" Then the odor reached me. Uh-oh, no playacting, this was the real thing.

"Hey! That's not funny!" I scooped up Mr. Little Stink and his siblings, popped them back into the cage, shoved in the cat food, and secured the door with a heavy box. I escaped into a crisp West Virginia morning scented with tulip magnolia blossoms, which I could no longer smell. Well, it wasn't much spray. Just a baby, not an adult. Plenty of time to change to a clean uniform for work.

As I fastened the shed door, a thought came to mind: *Baby skunks can spray!* So little skunks do smell bad—like "little" sins?

Uh-oh, Father, do I have any smelly "little" sins in my life? I remember self-pity, worry, criticism of others, a sharp tongue when tired. Ouch! Being faced with sin is never comfortable, but it is oh-so-nice to confess and stop doing it. I had a lot of "stinkies" to consider.

Checking the car clock, I sipped my coffee and noted that the smell was now faint—maybe just a little in my hair.

I grabbed my stethoscope and home-visit bag and reached the pharmacy's back office with one minute to spare.

"Good mornin'!" I said to the backs of secretaries and billing department ladies already working. I checked my patient visitation schedule. Marsha suddenly wheeled her office chair around. Bonnie glanced over her shoulder, face all scrunched up.

"Gal, what is that smell?" demanded Iris, holding files in front of her nose. Their eyes widened in disbelief as I related my morning adventure.

"You just can't smell yourself anymore," said Marsha, flapping billing sheets around her head. My nose was numb from the skunk chemicals. Their noses were not.

Bonnie giggled, "Can you just see her patients' faces if she came in like this? Wonder if they'd say anything, or pretend not to smell skunk." My homebound oxygen patients certainly wouldn't benefit from my new perfume.

The boss suggested I take the rest of the day off and pick up some tomato juice on the way home, please. He even offered to pay for it. The ladies volunteered to call my patients—anything to get me out of the pharmacy.

"Have a good day at home!" called Iris.

Marsha wiped tears from the corners of her eyes. "We haven't had a laugh like this in a long time! Now don't forget to stop at the food store, hon! Where's my can of air freshener?" She followed me out the front door, spraying as I went.

I noticed a few people in the grocery store looking puzzled when I passed. The Eau de Striped Kitty was still present. I hurried to the checkout.

The soak and scrub would have been downright revolting if I hadn't grabbed the tomato juice with oregano. Now

I smelled like pizza sauce. But sitting in a tub of red liquid was a great object lesson to finish up the "little skunk–little sins" illustration.

"What can wash away my sin? Nothing but the blood of Jesus. What can make me whole again? Nothing but the blood of Jesus."

It was a new perspective on being washed in my Lord's precious blood. He died and suffered for my "little" sins, too, the sins I often ignore and overlook. I may not be able to detect the smell of these sins, especially once I get accustomed to them, and I need the Holy Spirit to nudge me into repentance. Isaiah said, "Instead of smelling of sweet perfume, she will stink" (Isaiah 3:24).

Maybe the sins are baby sized, but they are still a stink in God's nostrils. Jesus' blood was shed to cleanse me from these sins too. And if I don't repent, others will surely notice sin, not holiness, in my life.

That baby skunk cost me a day's leave, but the benefits were great. God gave me an insight to 2 Corinthians 2:15, which says, "Our lives are a Christ-like fragrance rising up to God. But this fragrance is perceived differently by those who are being saved and by those who are perishing."

My new "perfume" also gave me an opportunity to tell the ladies at work the skunk story from God's viewpoint.

—Kathleen S. Rogers

THE CALL

What am I supposed to do with my life?

As a new Christian, that was a regular prayer on my lips. At first I thought God must want me to be a doctor because that was what I was preparing for in college before I'd become a Christian. However, I didn't really want to be a doctor.

Because of my newfound zeal for Christ, some of my friends and profs suggested I consider training for the ministry.

"The ministry?" I replied. "No way!"

As a non-Christian, the only ministers I had ever known were short, fat, bald, and boring. Even though the ministers I'd met after I got saved weren't like that, the image stuck. I didn't want to be the cause of someone's boredom or headache between eleven and twelve on Sunday.

Then God zapped me. One weekend, while working as a cook and ski instructor in Stratton, Vermont, I became depressed. I didn't know why I felt so out of sorts so I walked down to the little Chapel of the Snows, a nondenominational church center, to talk to the Lord about it.

A few minutes into the "discussion," a quiet voice seemed to speak inside my head: *I want you to go into the ministry!*

I was immediately stricken with mortal terror. *No way!*

That soon gave way to anger. I replied to that inner voice, *I can't go into the ministry. I don't know how to do it.*

It doesn't matter, the voice seemed to say.

This is a trick of the devil to get me more depressed, I replied.

The voice responded, *Would the devil want you to serve me?*

I didn't know what to answer to that, so I said, *Choose Tim, he's a great candidate for the ministry!* Tim was a coworker at the Liftline Lodge where I was a cook and dishwasher.

No, I want you, he insisted.

This scared me. I didn't want to be a minister. Ministers don't make much money. And anyway, I wanted to get married. What girl wanted to marry clergy?

The voice continued, *Mark, listen. You can do it. I'll be with you the whole way.*

I can't be a minister, I wailed in terror. *I don't know how to speak in public.*

The voice said, *I'll teach you!*

My fear of public speaking was deeply ingrained. In college I wouldn't even take classes that required any kind of speaking assignment.

The voice and I went back and forth like that for what seemed hours. In the end, though, I couldn't fight it. So I said, *All right, I'll be a minister. But you have to do some things for me. First of all, you'll have to show me that I can speak in public.*

I was convinced I had the Lord on that one.

Second, you'll have to show me I can lead people to Christ.

I'd never led anyone to the Lord at that point, and so believed I wasn't very good at it.

Third, I said, *you'll have to show me I can do counseling.*

I knew pastors and ministers did a lot of counseling, and I'd never even taken a psych course.

Finally, I intoned, sure God could not answer any of my

requests so far but needing a clincher, *you'll have to show me that being in the ministry will become the source of the greatest joy and fulfillment in my life.*

Now that was truly impossible. Who could make me want to do something I considered on a par with burger flipping at the local greasy spoon?

That finished, I waited, and the voice seemed to have faded into the woodwork. I said in my mind, *You can't do any of that, I bet.*

I went back to my apartment confident I'd gotten God off that track and off my back.

But I hadn't reckoned with the sovereign God of the universe, who specializes in the impossible.

One night I sat in the foyer of the restaurant where I worked, reading the Bible. A man walked over to me, scrutinized my Bible, and said, "Excuse me, are you a Jesus freak?"

I cleared my throat and said, "Yes, sort of, but I just like to call myself a Christian."

He said, "You know, I've heard about that. Would you tell me about it?"

This was a bit unusual, but I started giving him the details of how I had become a Christian. About three seconds into my speech, other members of his party showed up and he called them over. "Hey, listen to this guy. This is really interesting."

I stood up and continued, and as people moved in and out of the restaurant, several groups joined my little conclave. Soon, I had about twenty people standing around listening to my testimony. I was fully clothed, was still in my right mind, and had not slobbered or slithered off into the daisies. In fact, I was enjoying it!

I was amazed.

After I finished, the man thanked me, adding that I was a pretty good speaker and should consider the ministry. I remembered my prayer of several days before and said, *Lord, this isn't . . . No!*

I decided it was just coincidence.

Nonetheless, I couldn't shake off the realization of how much I'd enjoyed it. Speaking in front of those people didn't exhaust me; it enthralled me.

Still, that answered only one part of my prayer. Surely God couldn't . . .

A week later I was working in the kitchen with a coworker. This coworker, named Kris, hated me. She was living with a guy at the time. Her boyfriend, Joel, and I had many discussions about Christianity and why I believed premarital sex was wrong. She didn't like me "messing with Joel's mind," and she once threatened me with a knife, saying that if I didn't "lay off her boyfriend," she would "sneak into my room some night and cut me open like a Christmas turkey."

That didn't stop my conversations with Joel, though I avoided her as much as possible.

One afternoon Kris dashed into the kitchen scared out of her wits. Her ex-boyfriend had just showed up—the one who had always beat her. He'd been hired as the new staff handyman. Kris was terrified.

She spilled the whole story. I listened, and when she finished, I started in on my testimony about how becoming a Christian had changed everything and rid me of much of the fear I'd had in my B.C. (Before Christ) days. In the process, I shared the gospel. Finally I said, "Would you like to ask Jesus to come into your life?"

She answered, "I just did—while you were talking."

I was stunned. And then the little voice in my head reminded me, *By the way, that was the second part of your prayer, remember?*

I swallowed hard and tried not to think of where this was leading.

The next event occurred in the foyer again. I was sitting on a couch reading a Christian book, when a lady walked in from skiing and sat down on the couch opposite me. I continued reading, and suddenly she began weeping.

I put down the book and said, "Are you all right, ma'am?"

Clearly she wasn't. She said, "I noticed the book you're reading. Are you a Christian?"

I nodded, hoping this wouldn't lead to a harangue or something worse.

She went on, "I have such a problem in my life."

I put aside my book, and she began telling me how her college-graduate son had found himself caught up in the occult, suffered a mental breakdown, and ended up in a bad job. As she wept, I felt truly pained for her.

She looked at me with tear-filled eyes and said, "I just don't know what to do anymore. We came up here to try to have some fun and get away from it all, but I feel as bad as I ever did. Do you think you can help me?"

I didn't have a clue what to say, but I opened my Bible, thinking God would lead me to something pertinent. I had recently memorized Proverbs 3:5-6, and it occurred to me that might be a good starting point. I read it to her: "Trust in the LORD with all your heart; do not depend on your own understanding. Seek his will in all you do, and he will show you which path to take."

Then I began telling her what this Scripture meant and how it could help her through her problem. She listened intently and asked me questions. Answers mysteriously flooded my brain. As other texts came to mind, I showed them to her, and we talked more about her son. It was a marvelous time of fellowship and friendship. When she had to go because her family walked in, we prayed together.

And then she dropped the bomb. She said, "You know, you're really good. You should be a counselor."

As she left, smiling, I sat there absolutely knocked off my feet. God had done it! The first three prayers had been answered. I had discovered I could speak in public after all. I could lead people to Christ. And I could counsel. And then, even more amazing, I realized I was energized and encouraged and spiritually strengthened by all these new experiences. I was happy and excited. I'd never felt so good! That was the fourth requirement checked off my list.

The reality of it all filled me, and I sat there, too amazed to speak. But finally I said, *OK, God, you win. I'll go into the ministry.*

Tears burned my eyes. I was relieved. My greatest question about the purpose of my life on earth had been answered. I'd only been a Christian for five months, and though that's been about thirty years ago now, I've spent the decades immersed in ministry.

Back then I learned that when we're wondering what God has for us, we simply need to open our hearts to him, listen, and wait. He'll amaze us—maybe even for the rest of our lives!

—**Mark R. Littleton**

THE TURTLEDOVE RESCUE BLESSING

Like a guard at Buckingham Palace, the turtledove remained stationary on the church lawn. As my son Karl and I approached, we expected it to fly away. Instead, it stubbornly remained in place. It didn't seek food, eat, or move. It stood gazing on some object.

In true eight-year-old-boy form, Karl briefly charged in the bird's direction to startle it. It didn't budge. When we started to climb the stairs into the building, I realized the reason for its persistent immobility: There, on the second step, was a fluffy, gray and white turtledove chick hopping about, shedding down and leaving little nervous "deposits."

We gave a wide berth to the chick while I took Karl to his classroom and got him settled. On the way to my class, I checked on the chick again. I noticed another turtledove and chick also nearby—hidden in the shadow behind a twisted evergreen tree. The devoted family would wait close at hand until someone, somehow, rescued its little one.

"There's a baby bird stuck out on the stairs," I told my husband, Gary, who was busy making coffee for our couples' class.

He looked at me quizzically. "And?"

"I want to help it," I said. "How do I help it?"

He began to answer when someone else walked in, a new father who needed coffee and Gary's listening ear. In the large scheme of things, I knew my query about the bird was less important than his friend's immediate need. I would ask again later.

Meanwhile, I looked around the room for something, anything, to help me help the little bird. I remembered hearing that you should never touch a baby bird. First, it often had germs and bugs. Second, I heard that the human smell on the bird could turn its parents against it. I checked the pockets of my sweater. Why didn't I have my gloves with me? I knew it was May and forecast to be a warm day, but gloves would have done the trick.

On a counter, I saw some floppy, multicolored game disks the size of small plates. Perhaps I could slide one of these under the bird and move it? But they were so flexible that if the chick panicked, it could fall and be worse off than it was before. I looked at the coffee cups. They weren't much bigger than the chick. If I stuffed the little thing in one of them to move it, its anxiety might escalate and the poor baby could have a heart attack. Maybe if I used a combination of a Styrofoam cup and a plate? The cup could guide the baby onto the plate, and then I could carry it over to its family. But what if it pecked at me and I dropped the plate?

"I'm going to check on the bird again," I announced to Gary and whoever else might wonder where I was going.

On my way out of the classroom I saw our teacher, Ken, approaching from the parking lot.

"There's a baby bird in trouble," I said. Maybe he would have the solution. Ken followed me, and I pointed out the chick and its anxious family.

As I waited for wise counsel from my bewildered teacher—I could see he was wondering why I had called him over to see the baby bird's predicament—two men emerged from the door behind the stairs. In about ten seconds, one of the men, the building manager, sized up the situation. He set down the things he was carrying and said, "Let's take care of this problem."

He gently picked up the little bird, talking all the while in low tones, and then put it down near the parent. Then he headed off to wash his hands, and the rescued chick hopped away to join its family.

Forty-five minutes later, after class, I checked the scene again. Both turtledoves and both chicks were nowhere in sight. Their family had been restored and they had moved on.

I could have had a part in that. I could have rescued the chick. And I could have done it fifteen minutes earlier. Instead, I had agonized about the right way to save the chick and so did nothing.

I started thinking, *How often do I spend my time and effort trying to figure out the best methods, the proper techniques, the perfect words until I lose the moment to actually do anything? How often do I lose the potential blessings that God puts in my path?*

I recalled a hurting acquaintance I had spoken to recently. I kept wondering if she was a huggy type of person, and not wishing to offend, I never offered the physical reassurance she needed. Another friend came up moments later, saw the teary eyes, and gave her the hug I could have provided.

Or what about the waitress who commented on my praying before a meal? She asked if I always did that and opened a huge door for me to talk about my faith. I considered the right thing to say for so long that her free moment disappeared in the lunch rush, and I could only call out a feeble "God bless you!" as I left the restaurant.

Even more agonizing, I thought of the letter I had written to my sick aunt. I knew she did not attend church or believe in much of anything. I had witnessed to her before and had felt belittled for it. So in this letter, wanting to say just the right thing to make her feel appreciated, I "soft soaped" the Good News. I wrote "God bless you" and "I'm praying for you" but filled the rest of the letter with small talk and encouragement to get well.

That was the last time I wrote to her before she died. I could have spelled out the gospel in a few words or put a tract inside the card. I could have given her another chance to receive the truth. Instead, at her memorial service, friends praised her commitment to atheism. Would things have changed if I had followed the Spirit's leading? Perhaps not. But my own soul would have the comfort of knowing that I did what I had been called to do.

That morning God had given me the opportunity to help a baby turtledove. And he had given me two very washable hands to help it with. As I looked at the corner of the second step, still decorated with wisps of turtledove down, I asked him for the strength and boldness to act the next time.

Father God, remind me that you did not create me to do things perfectly but to do what you ask me to do. Fill me with heavenly courage and wisdom. Amen.

—Susan A. J. Lyttek

COLLECTIVE STUPIDITY

Romans 7:15, 18-19 comes to parents' minds many times when they have three sons: "I don't really understand myself, for I want to do what is right . . . but I can't. . . . I don't want to do what is wrong, but I do it anyway."

A friend of mine told me about a theorem called the Law of Collective Stupidity. An adaptation of this principle states that among people who are of nonadult age, the degree of stupidity increases in direct proportion to the number of people gathered together. In other words, the more kids you have in one place, the more likely they are to do something really dumb.

I believe this especially applies to those of the male gender.

When boys congregate, they manage to do things that most of them would never do if they were alone. Perhaps the concentration of testosterone increases their adrenaline, which compels them to do something—anything—that sounds bold and brave. Maybe the presence of other boys gives them the courage to try things they would never have attempted on their own. Or maybe God made them that way (on purpose?).

Whether the reasons are biological, sociological, or

pathological, boys feel constrained to find new and thrilling ways to impress their peers. When you question them about their antics—"What were you thinking?"—they respond, with absolute honesty, "I dunno."

The sad truth is, they really don't know. One boy comes up with an idea. Another boy says, "Cool!" And boy brain cells start to die.

A case in point: When my firstborn was about thirteen, we left him in charge of his brothers (ages eleven and eight) while my husband and I were out for the day. Josh was a thoughtful, intelligent boy that any mother would be proud to claim. Conscientious. Trustworthy. Sensible.

Until that day.

For some unfathomable reason, he decided it would be a good idea to invite a friend over while we were gone. Hey—why not two or three friends! The more the merrier, right? Of course, he didn't bother informing their mothers that no adult would be home for the next six or seven hours.

So Josh and Jason and Michael, our beloved progeny, gathered in the living room with Chris, Chad, and Cody, our neighbors. They looked around the room. They looked at one another. They looked at the second-story loft bedroom that overlooked the living room.

"I know what we can do!" exclaimed some clever fellow whose identity has never been revealed. "Let's pile all the furniture cushions under the loft, and let's jump down onto them."

The other boys thought this was an inspired idea. They took every cushion from the couch and loveseat, plus all the pillows and blankets, and created a mountain of polyester foam. Then they trooped upstairs and, one by one, took a flying leap.

To their boyish delight, their idea worked. What a grand time they had falling from the loft, landing on the mound of pillows, and scurrying back upstairs for another turn.

Did any of them consider that the pile of pillows could unexpectedly shift and someone could land, smack, on the floor?

Did any of them ponder the proposal and think, *Hmm, I don't think Mother would appreciate us jumping on her furniture?*

Did any of them think about the fact that their landing pad was mere inches from a natural stone fireplace? If one of them had jumped too far out instead of straight down, he could have cracked a skull, or worse. (I seriously doubt, however, that the injured boy would have suffered any brain damage; anyone jumping from the loft didn't have any brains in the first place.)

The answer to all three questions is—haha—of course not! None of them thought about the consequences because none of them thought, period. You had six boys together with no adult supervision. Someone was bound to come up with a very bad idea that sounded like a lot of fun. And because of the Law of Collective Stupidity, none of the other boys would point out any flaws because none of the boys would see any flaws.

My husband and I did not learn of the Loft Leaping Exercise for months. In fact, we did not learn of it until we were ready to move out of that house and the boys apparently felt it was now safe to reveal the adventure. By then, they had hosted several more Loft Leaps.

Sometimes I think God must look at us the way I viewed my boys that day. What was patently obvious to me—leaping from a second-story loft is stupid and dangerous—was not so obvious to my boys.

How many times have I done something that was just as stupid? Maybe not physically dangerous like jumping from a loft, but something that would put my spiritual well-being at risk. How many times have I ignored the warning signs God has posted, determined to forge ahead and do what I wanted to do regardless of the consequences? And how many times has God been there to help me pick up the pieces and start over when my disobedience created a disaster?

I learned two important lessons from this experience: First, God is a patient, loving Father who forgives me my shortcomings just as I forgave my foolish boys. Sometimes when I'm about to do something foolish, he stops me short by bringing those Loft Leaps to my mind.

The second thing I learned is that a boy must never, under any circumstances, be left with other boys until he moves out of the house and into his own place.

And then I'm coming over to jump on *his* furniture.

—Rhonda Wheeler Stock

CRUNCH-TIME MIRACLE

After years of saving and searching, we had just purchased a new home in our little storybook town. Even though we stretched a bit further than was financially conservative, we delighted in grand plans to freshen up the shabby cottage. We were enchanted by the backyard, which stretched out in a full half-acre, wooded park, complete with twinkling fireflies and a gurgling creek.

Then came September 11, 2001, and the terrorist attacks in the United States. Once the economy felt the full impact of that dreadful day, we knew that our highly specialized businesses would suffer. We fought to keep our new home, yet our struggling income simply wouldn't support our mortgage. Finally, we listed our dreamy homesite, and after tense months of stalling creditors and foreclosure, a buyer appeared, right before Christmas.

The original closing date was set for late January. We began to look for a new residence, but our fairy-tale village boosted its image most effectively in its price point. Real estate was expensive, and rent followed suit. We had a few weeks, so we weren't panicked, although many nights I lay awake trying to figure out how to design a tent that would house us, our two toddlers, and a generator to run the computers for both of our home-based businesses. Unfortunately, even the tent was out of our price range!

A few days after signing the initial contracts, we learned of an agreement made between the realtors, where our agent—aware of our pressing financial situation—agreed to close three weeks earlier than originally planned. Our kind and trustworthy agent, distracted with a sudden family emergency, failed to tell us this detail.

The buying family had already made contracts to relinquish their property by the new date, so there was no going back. And as we had already committed to a weeklong holiday with family in another part of the state, this left us with roughly one week to find a suitable place to live and to vacate the premises.

At this shocking news, my husband and I decided to take a drive. We rode in distressed silence until my husband found a place to pull over. He took my hands, and together we approached the Throne.

"Father," he began, "how well you know our situation. We are up against the proverbial wall, and we are looking up. You are our Provider, and we know that you have prepared a home for us. We are willing to do the work, to move at your command. We rest in your peace and thank you for your miracle in advance."

Slowly, quietly, a voice whispered in my head, *Call Mary*. I tried dismissing the thought, mistaking it for a low-priority item trying to jump ahead on my full to-do list. As I prepared to avoid my flesh pattern of going full speed ahead into a multitasking "divide and conquer" mode, the peaceful murmur, while only audible in my heart, impressed itself deeply: *Call Mary*. I shared this with my husband, and we headed home to obey at once.

About my mother's age, Mary was a delightful and dear friend, although we hadn't spoken in months. Our husbands had known each other years earlier while working together on a local charity project. After that, the four of us had attended personal-growth retreats together and had been witness and support to immeasurable spiritual growth. Despite the gap in our ages and financial fitness, our respect and love was mutual. They owned a business in a distant city, and to my knowledge they didn't dabble in local real estate, so I assumed they would be a source of prayer and possibly contacts for us.

Upon returning home to embark on our mission, I found a voice mail message from Mary on my home phone. Because it had been months since we had corresponded, my husband and I looked at each other, amazed by God's grace and kind confirmation. I called Mary immediately, going through the normal pleasantries and answering the questions from the voice mail.

"So," she said easily, "now catch me up. What is happening in your lives?"

In a lighthearted way, I asked, "Well, do you know anyone in town with way-below-market-price rental property?"

Considering the tone of our conversation, the absurdity of the question, and our manner of jesting and joking, I expected her to laugh. Instead, the line went silent. "I just might," she blurted. "I'll call you right back."

Fifteen long minutes later, she did just that. Hurriedly, she asked, "Can you meet me at this address in about half an hour?" Surprised that Karl and Mary would own rental property, and even more so that it would be vacant, we readily agreed.

We toured the three-bedroom home a bit dejectedly. It

was so nice—too nice for our budget, we knew. The established neighborhood, well-manicured yard, spacious living areas and bathrooms all spoke to its value. We began to tell them that although this was kind of them, we couldn't accept.

Karl and Mary explained that they had no interest in keeping rental property. They were too busy with other business and volunteer ventures, and the rental industry held no significance for them. However, over the previous year or so, they kept hearing of people in their church or in other ministries coming into unforeseen circumstances that warranted a quick sale, quick purchase, or—like us—quick rent of a home.

Suddenly, they had found themselves in a home ministry that, when governed by the Holy Spirit, proved to be most rewarding. This very home was purchased originally for a man in their church with advanced stages of diabetes. Originally a rancher, the debilitated man needed a home in town so that he could get his son to school and make it to the hospital for dialysis in his severely weakened condition. Unfortunately, the rancher passed away, and his son moved in with relatives.

At the very moment that I had obeyed the Lord's quiet whisper that said, *Call Mary,* Karl was on his way to his realtor's office to list the house for sale. Their purpose for the house was finished, and they weren't interested in a rental investment. Then we called, and they were guided back into their home ministry again.

Karl began discussing monthly rental fees at half of what we had been paying in mortgage installments. That was impossible in this market! It was about what my tent would've cost! Even after protesting that they would have plenty of takers at nearly twice the price, they would have none of it.

We accepted, so humbled, so grateful and amazed at God's provision.

When we returned from our weeklong holiday, our new home had been completely repainted and recarpeted, and the new kitchen appliances sparkled. The home fit our family like a glove. Even the yard, though not a park, amply provided a garden, flower beds, peach trees, and plenty of play space for our children. The house needed no fixing up, and the efficient floor plan felt more spacious than our "dreamy cottage." We had almost no repair worries, one-tenth the yard work, more usable space, and half the expenses every month.

We have lived in this house for more than two years now, and fall more in love with it every day. Our livelihood has turned around with the recovered economy, and our faith and our gratitude grow daily as we bask in his glory and in our crunch-time miracle.

—Aimee Martin

FINDING THE BURNING BUSH

All my life, I'd wanted to see a "burning bush" from God. I asked other people if they'd ever seen such a spectacle of God's power. Some told me about falling down, great winds, and other amazing dramatic spiritual experiences. Why couldn't I have such an experience too? I wanted God to appear to me as, in the third chapter of Exodus, he'd appeared to Moses. I wanted to know that God had a purpose for me, too.

That's the stage of my spiritual life I was in when, nearing sixty, I joined a missions trip to Honduras. I had gone twice before as part of a construction team. On those trips, I learned to build chicken coops and septic systems. This trip's emphasis—evangelism—was something new, different, and a bit scary for me.

The fifteen in our group from the U.S. were teamed with fifteen Hondurans. Every morning we piled into a van and trucks for a ninety-minute ride into the mountains. As the sun rose higher, so did the temperature. The tires kicked up dust behind us as we bumped past agricultural land and then mountainous terrain.

The local minister told us that when he was growing up in this area, the rains came in May. Now they came in July or later, and drought conditions were setting in. Drought's companions—poverty and hunger—could be close behind.

When we reached our destination, we divided into pairs like the disciples Jesus sent out in Luke 10:1. Two by two, one American and one Honduran, we knocked on doors. The typical small, rural village consisted of cinder-block homes with corrugated tin roofs. Some residents brought benches outside for us to sit on as we talked with them. A schoolteacher asked us into her home and gave us a refreshing drink. We invited all of the villagers to come to a "happening" at the school for the next four nights. We also told them about the games, songs, and stories available in the afternoons for their children.

The village families readily accepted our invitation. Each evening, we followed a similar pattern. The Hondurans sang with gusto, accompanied by guitars; fiddles, including a homemade bass fiddle; and an accordion. They chose songs that everyone knew or could learn easily. They didn't care if anyone was off key—the important thing was making a joyful noise. All of us together, still in our work clothes, made lots of it.

We foreign team members performed a different skit each night. Most of the skits were pantomime, with some Spanish words. Both Honduran and American team members gave testimonies. Sometimes some of us spoke Spanish, but usually we Americans spoke English. The minister translated for the audience. We showed the JESUS video in Spanish, and one of the ministers or a Honduran team member preached a short sermon. Most of all, we had fun singing and interacting.

The audience grew every night. On the second and third nights, the cinder-block schoolhouse was full. People squeezed together on benches beneath bare lightbulbs hanging from the ceiling. They crowded into the back and sides of the building. People stood outside in the darkness near the doors and windows on both sides of the schoolhouse. By the fourth night, people stuck their heads in the windows so they could participate.

That night, the minister invited anyone who wanted to dedicate or rededicate his or her life to Christ to come forward. About twelve to fifteen women and one man from the next village moved toward the front.

I watched from the back corner. The ministers advanced down the line, laid their hands on the people, and prayed over them. Something had changed in me during these four days of activity. I had always thought of God as the Father, and I knew that Jesus was God's son. I worshiped Father, Son, and Holy Spirit. The idea of dedicating my life to Christ had never occurred to me. Now, it was something I yearned to do. Self-consciousness held me back.

I stood in the corner and thought, *Don't be ridiculous, Tucker. Don't make a spectacle of yourself.* My feet froze to the tile floor.

Then I felt a very large hand settle on my back and push me forward. Before I knew it, I had walked toward the front and stood in line. When the minister came by, she prayed over the lady on my right. She started past me to the lady on my left.

"Wait," I said. "I would like to dedicate my life to Jesus Christ." She laid hands on me and prayed. I stood there with all those Hondurans, feeling wonderfully blessed.

When I got home, I talked about my experiences to a woman from our mission organization. She interrupted me when I told her the name of the place where we'd stayed, Corral Quemado. "You know what that means, don't you?" the woman asked.

"Yeah, it means 'burned,'" I said, remembering how hot and dry it was. "It's an appropriate name for the place."

"Yes, it means burned," the woman said, "but in some areas of the Spanish-speaking world, it's also the word used in the Bible to refer to the burning bush that Moses saw."

Not only had I seen the burning bush, I had lived in it for several days! God's hand had pushed me forward. I knew he'd given me a purpose, and my road has been different ever since.

Later, as a missionary in Honduras with the South American Missionary Society, I organized and oriented the same kinds of short-term mission groups I'd been part of. I prayed that they would see the burning bush too.

Now retired and back in the U.S., I marvel at how God was with me all along. He revealed himself in the hearts of the work teams. They provided medical and dental assistance, built churches and classrooms, donated Bibles, and offered hope and love. They sacrificed time, money, and energy to help others. One visiting veterinarian even sacrificed the tip of his finger when a horse bit it off!

When the hired bus of one of the medical teams died along the way, the team carried supplies the last several miles to their assigned mountain village. They found several hundred people waiting for care. Rather than rest, the team set up and got right to work.

Honduras was still recovering from Hurricane Mitch, so teams restored a church and improved its safety by building a seawall, resetting a septic system, and securing the building's footings.

God also revealed himself in the hospitality of the Hondurans, their eager desire for the gospel, and their gratitude for assistance. At many sites where teams worked, local people—including children—pitched in. In one area, people went without food in order to donate money to have their own building of worship. One group of Honduran women raised money for their church by selling food at fiestas and fixing up old bicycles to sell.

God was certainly with me as I drove back and forth to the airport to pick up teams. After airport security tightened, though no one else was allowed inside to pick up passengers, we were able to go inside to meet our groups and lead them through customs. Even when a new government came into power and exercised its ability to demand more detailed paperwork before teams arrived, no team member was ever turned away!

I saw God in the beauty of Honduras, where the air was sometimes heavy with the scent of tropical flowers. The coastal waters sparkled blue-green, and the mountains jutted toward the sky. The people with whom I worked and lived created community among strangers. They helped me understand local customs and language and forgave my mistakes. This could have happened only because of God's presence.

The bush still burns in my heart and my life. Having lived in different cultures in different places, I have come to know that wherever I'm standing, when God's work is going on, I'm on holy ground.

—Tucker Heitman, as told to Jane Heitman

MEET THE CONTRIBUTORS

Sandi Banks is mom to six children, grandma to ten, and gave birth to her first book, *Anchors of Hope,* in 2002. Other published contributions include stories in *Reader's Digest* and the Kisses of Sunshine series.

Gena Bradford, freelance writer, songwriter, retreat speaker, and worship leader, has been published in anthologies, periodicals, and recordings. Her latest CD, *Given Wings,* can be found at her web site: www.genabradford.com.

Laura L. Bradford spent thirty years as the primary caregiver for her disabled husband. It was a job she couldn't have undertaken aside from God's guidance and provision. Now she longs to let the world know about the tender care that God is faithful to provide to the hurting soul.

Dori Clark, married forty-six years to Duane, is the mother of three and grandmother of eight. A member of Oregon Christian Writers, she has written devotions, articles, and stories for numerous publications including the Cup of Comfort series.

Sally Clark and her husband, Mike, have retired after sixteen years in the restaurant business. They live in Fredericksburg, Texas, where Sally writes poetry, children's stories, humor, greeting cards, and creative non-fiction. She faithfully sends out Christmas cards every year. You may contact her at auslande@ktc.com.

Linda Crow is a wife, mother of three teenagers, and works in a youth ministry in Muncie, Indiana. She writes an occasional column for the local newspaper and enjoys blogging.

Cynthia L. D'Agostino is a mother of five and grandmother of two. She and her husband, Paul, are raising their children in Independence, Missouri. Cynthia enjoys her family, her friends, and all of their stories.

Brad Dixon has served in Christian ministry for over thirty years, and he now helps believers with practical questions about generosity. He's married, with three adult children, and looks forward to continuing to learn and grow.

Liz Hoyt Eberle writes about everyday people who often do not see that God uses their struggles and joys to bless others' lives. The stories she weaves have been widely published. She loves hearing from readers and can be contacted at eberle2@hotmail.com.

Melissa Fields is originally a Southern girl from Walton, West Virginia. She graduated from the University of Central Florida before beginning a magazine publishing career in New England. She currently homeschools her two wonderful children as they prayerfully await her husband's return from Iraq.

Evangeline Beals Gardner is a stay-at-home mom who teaches piano lessons and does freelance writing projects on the side. Her two daughters, ages eleven and eighteen, keep her household full of life, energy, and excitement. She enjoys being a praise and worship leader at her church and leading a Bible study in her home.

Sandra Glahn writes, teaches classes at Dallas Theological Seminary, and edits the seminary's magazine, *Kindred Spirit.*

Helen Heavirland has been published in a variety of magazines and anthologies and has written three books. She practices thankfulness from her home in Oregon.

Jane Heitman writes for educational and Christian publications, including several Cup of Comfort compilations.

Tucker Heitman served in Honduras with the South American Missionary Society of the Episcopal church. Now retired, she lives in Illinois.

Linda Holloway's education career spanned over thirty years. She has written articles for *Rare Jewel Magazine, SpiritLed Woman,* and *MetroVoice.* She contributed to three *Ministry in the 21st Century* books by Group Publishing.

Cindy Hval's work has appeared in a variety of compilations. She's a correspondent for the *Spokesman Review* newspaper in Spokane, Washington, where she and her husband are raising their four sons. Contact her at dchval@juno.com.

Michael J. Keown holds a master's degree in education and certification in school administration. After thirty-three years in public education as a teacher and school administrator, he retired to begin his writing career. He lives in Arlington, Oregon, with his wife and three dogs.

Laurie Klein's stories appear in a variety of journals and anthologies. A cofounder and consulting editor of *Rock & Sling: A Journal of Literature, Art and Faith,* she also wrote the classic contemporary chorus "I Love You, Lord."

Ardythe Kolb and her husband have five grown children and seven grandchildren. They owned and operated a successful Christian bookstore for thirteen years. After they sold the store, Ardythe worked as a church secretary until she retired and started writing. She enjoys spending time with her family, travel, reading, and volunteer work for Heart of America Christian Writers Network and Prison Fellowship.

Mark R. Littleton is the author of more than ninety books. His most recent titles include *101 Amazing Truths about Jesus That You Probably Didn't Know* and *The Ten-Second Prayer Principles.* Mark is also available for speaking at conferences, churches, retreats, as well as other meetings. You can contact him at mlittleton@earthlink.net.

Kevin Lucia writes for the *Press & Sun Bulletin* and his short fiction has appeared in the journal *Relief & Coach's Midnight Diner*. He holds a bachelor's degree in English and teaches high school honors English. He and his wife, Abby; daughter, Madison; and son, Zackary, live in Castle Creek, New York.

Susan A. J. Lyttek, wife of Gary since 1983 and homeschool mother of two boys, Erik and Karl, has published everything from plays to greeting cards to medical articles and devotions. She writes and teaches writing online through WriteAtHome from the suburbs of our nation's capital . . . and before the boys wake up.

Aimee Martin still lives in her miracle home in Fredericksburg, Texas, with her husband and two small children. She writes mostly Christian nonfiction with heart-warming, lesson-laden messages. She loves hearing from readers and may be contacted at aimeebrints@yahoo.com.

Elaine Young McGuire, a retired educator and grandmother of five, lives with her husband of forty-three years and cat, Max, in Lilburn, Georgia. She loves mission work and writing stories that glorify God, because he has done so much for her. Her published work has appeared in various periodicals and anthologies.

Lisa McKay is a pastor's wife and mother of four in Alabama. She loves to teach God's Word to women through speaking events. Lisa also writes online Bible studies and other pieces of encouragement on her blog, The Preacher's Wife, at www.thepreachers-wife.blogspot.com.

Lucy Michaels is the pseudonym for an author who has written a booklet for the Church and Synagogue Library Association, another book about a Christian author, has taught in college and high school, and has worked as a reference librarian.

Peggy Overstreet is the assistant athletic director at Cascade Christian High School in Jacksonville, Oregon. As a writer, she finds inspiration living in the beautiful Rogue River Valley of Southern Oregon.

Leslie J. Payne is a retired sign language interpreter for the deaf. She and husband Richard are grateful for every day of their married life. They live in Annapolis, Maryland, and enjoy family, travel, and sailing their boat *New Life.*

Jim Rawdon, a native of the western Oklahoma prairies, has experience as a chef and in a men's clothing business. At age forty he became a pastor and, seventeen years later, began writing.

Vivian Reed lives in Long Beach, California, where she's currently transitioning into a full-time writing career. She is proud to write the "Recognitions" column for *T-Zero: The Writers' E-zine.*

Eileen Roddy-Phillips is a pastoral consultant and author living in Lawrence, Kansas, with her husband, Don.

Kathleen S. Rogers lives with her family in the mountains of West Virginia, where she writes, home educates, hunts, and dabbles with artist trading cards. A member of Bethany Fellowship, Kathee loves to communicate about God's priceless redemption through the Lord Jesus Christ.

Rhonda Wheeler Stock has been a freelance writer for sixteen years. She has been a humor columnist for *Today's Christian Woman* and has written articles and curriculum. She and her husband live in Kansas and are the parents of three boys and a girl. Rhonda teaches junior high special education and enjoys prowling around flea markets, thrift stores, and antique shops.

Dennis Stout is a veteran youth minister. He and his family live in the Kansas City area, where he ministers to students and adults in various ways.

Donna Sundblad, lives in Georgia with her husband, Rick. Her writing covers how-to books, inspirational works, and fantasy. Her books *Pumping Your Muse* and *Windwalker* are available at epress-online.com. Check out her website at www.theinkslinger.net for more information.

Ann Varnum is hostess of *The Ann Varnum Show,* which airs weekdays on WTVY-TV in Dothan, Alabama. She is also a freelance writer and has a devotional series which airs weekdays on AFR affiliate WAQG in Alabama.

Tamara Vermeer has a background in journalism and marketing and lives in Colorado with her husband and three children. She is an avid reader with a heart for reaching out to women through Bible studies, writing, and coffee.

Rachel Wallace-Oberle has an education in journalism and in radio and television broadcasting, and she writes for numerous publications and The Foundation for International Development Assistance. She is also a founding member of Faith FM 94.3, the first Christian radio station in Kitchener-Waterloo, Ontario. She lives with her husband and two sons and loves walking, classical music, and canaries.

Emily Tipton Williams is a freelance writer and violinist. She serves as a spiritual director and lay minister in the Episcopal church in Fort Worth, Texas. Emily's novel, *Restless Soul,* takes place in Great Britain, one of her frequent travel destinations. She and her husband, Mike, have five children and four grandchildren.

ABOUT THE AUTHORS

JAMES STUART BELL

James Stuart Bell is the owner of Whitestone Communications, a literary development agency. He consults with numerous publishers, represents various authors, and provides writing and editing services. He has previously served as executive editor at Moody Press, director of religious publishing at Doubleday, and publisher at Bridge Publishing. He coauthored the best-selling *Complete Idiot's Guide to the Bible* and numerous other Christian guides in that section for the Penguin Group. He has also contributed numerous Christian volumes to the best-selling Cup of Comfort series by Adams Media.

JEANETTE GARDNER LITTLETON

Jeanette Gardner Littleton, the author of about a dozen books including *When Your Teen Goes Astray: Help and Hope from Parents Who've Been There*, has thirty years' experience in the writing and editing fields. She has been on the editorial staff of eight publications, including *Moody Magazine*, and has written several thousand articles. A freelance writer and editor, she is content editor/consultant for several Christian publications, is a series editor for Barbour, and edits for other book publishers. Jeanette and her husband, Mark, share a passion for encouraging and equipping Christian writers as co-directors of Heart of America Christian Writers Network.